W9-CHH-092

JOHN DEERE GENERAL–PURPOSE

Tractors

JOHN DEERE

New "A" and "B" Series

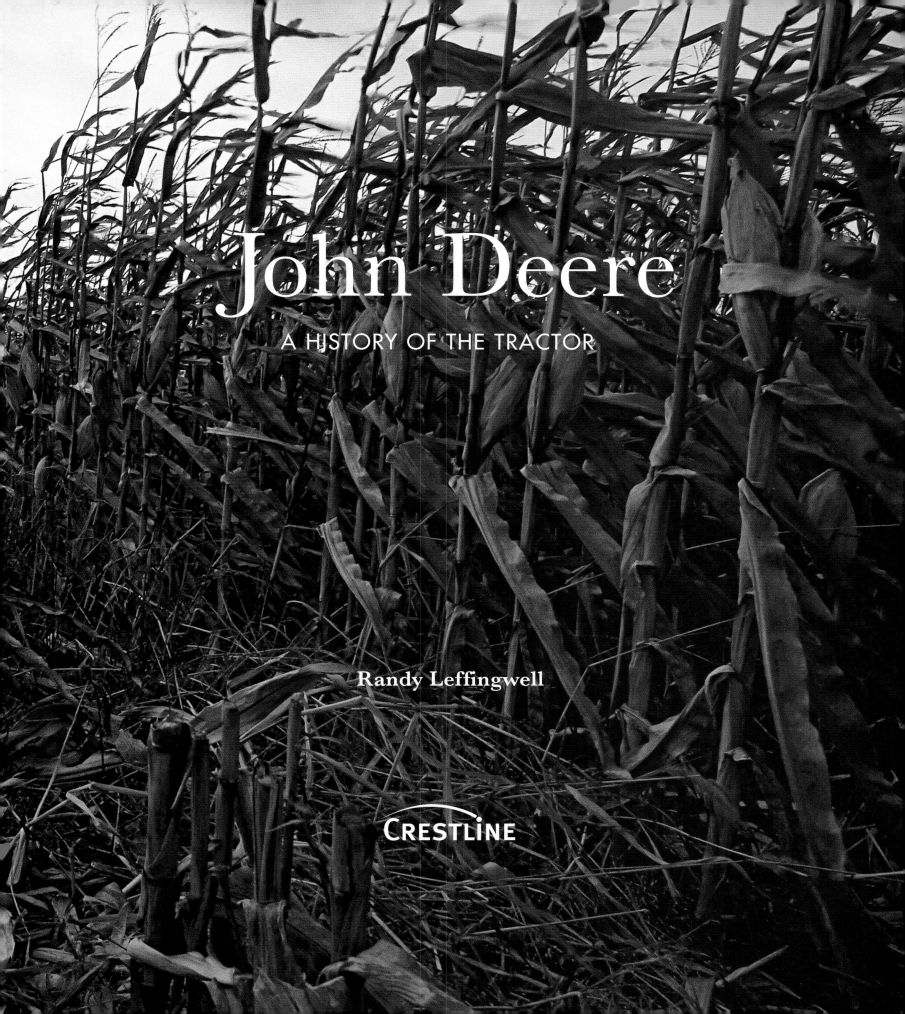

John Deere

A HISTORY OF THE TRACTOR

Randy Leffingwell

CRESTLINE

On the cover: The 20 Series, including this 1957 620 Hi-Crop, came standard with Custom Powr-Trol and live PTO, each of which operated independently of the transmission clutch.

On the frontispiece: This Deere & Company brochure promoted the company's new Model A and B tractors.

On the title page: Model G Hi-Crops were built only from 1951 through mid-January 1953. This 1953 Hi-Crop, number 63,674, was originally shipped to Louisiana just after New Years where many Hi-Crop tractors ended up working in cotton and sugar cane fields. Electric start and headlights were standard.

On the back cover: The all-fuel Model 70 was powered by the 6.125x7.00-inch engine that produced 31.1 drawbar horsepower at 975 rpm. The pulley produced 38.4 horsepower. A new combustion-chamber design was introduced, the "cyclonic fuel intake," which swirled the fuel mixture cyclone-like for better combustion and economy.

Contents

Acknowledgments

This book benefited greatly from the Deere & Company historical photographs and historical perspective provided by Leslie Stegh, Archivist, Deere & Company, Moline, Illinois.

William Hewitt, Chadds Ford, Pennsylvania, Chairman of Deere & Company from 1955 to 1982, was exceptionally generous with his time and insights.

Russell Flinchum, New York, New York, has dedicated years to researching Henry Dreyfuss and his work. He unhesitatingly shared his extraordinary research.

Jim Connor, Old Greenwich, Connecticut, and Bill Purcell, Tiverton, Massachusetts, both retired Henry Dreyfuss Associates partners, explained the design philosophy, perspectives, and accomplishments.

Bill Figart, General Manager, Gary LaBouff, Engineer, and Bob Osborn, Vice-President, all of Rotary Power International, filled in the knowledge of Deere & Company's experiments in rotary power.

The late Jesse G. Lindeman, Yakima, Washington, enthusiastically and painstakingly provided the history of his crawlers. Ted Adams, Manager, Lindex, arranged the interviews and let me pour through Lindeman archives and copy many photos.

Jack Cherry, President, Two-Cylinder Club, opened files and shared the insights of his late father, Lyle Cherry, former sales manager, Waterloo Plant, Deere & Company. This overview was invaluable.

My thanks to Larry Armstrong, Bob Chamberlin, and Cindy Hively, Los Angeles Times Photo Assignment Desk, for allowing me the time to do this book. My further thanks to MBI, for suggesting the idea and allowing me to do it.

Without the love and devotion of the collectors themselves, much of our agricultural history would have gone to the scrap heap. This book honors their vision:

Ken Berns, Blue Hill, Nebraska; Harold Chilcote, Greencastle, Indiana; Paul Cook, Yakima, Washington; Tony Dieter, Vail, Iowa; Don and Sylvia Dufner, Buxton, North Dakota; Frank and Irene Hansen, Altura, Minnesota; Bruce Henderson, Charter Oak, Iowa; Maurice Horn, Rochester, Indiana; Colin Johnson, Albert City, Iowa; Kenny Kass, Dunkerton, Iowa; Bruce and Judy Keller, Brillion, Wisconsin; Walter Keller, Kaukauna, Wisconsin; Jack Kreeger, Omaha, Nebraska; Lester, Kenny, and Harland Layher, Wood River, Nebraska; Larry and Melanie Maasdam, Clarion, Iowa; Scott McAllister, Mount Pleasant, Iowa; Don and Greg Merrihew, Mount Pleasant, Michigan; Harv Monesmith, Bourbon, Indiana; Robert and Mary Pollock, Denison, Iowa; Arlo Schoenfeld, Charter Oak, Iowa; Harold Schultz, Ollie, Iowa; and Barry and Jeannette Stelford, Urbana, Illinois.

To all of you who fitted up implements, touched up paint, loaded or unloaded transporters, spun flywheels, got up early, missed meals, and introduced me to others who would do the same, I cannot thank you enough. I hope you enjoy the fruits of your labor.

Randy Leffingwell
Los Angeles, California

With a coffee can protecting the exhaust pipe from coming rain, this Model BNH, number 87,784, rests silhouetted on a hilltop near Denison, Iowa.

Introduction
"Not Content To Be Runner-Up"

For Deere & Company, one historically significant event was never recorded on any calendar. The day on which it occurred began inauspiciously. It was just another day in the early 1950s.

It was not the day William Alexander Hewitt received a phone call from his father-in-law, Colonel Charles Deere ("The Colonel") Wiman, offering him the most important job at Deere & Company.

Hewitt remembered that day the date, the hour, and his response.

"Well, Sir," he politely said. "I'm very grateful and very flattered. It's quite an honor. What I'd like to do is to talk to Tish about it."

Tish Hewitt was born Patricia Wiman. Although she had married Deere & Company's youngest —and first-ever executive vice president, she was still the daughter of the Colonel.

"I already have," the Colonel quickly replied, expecting from Dewitt an equally quick reaction.

And so, William Alexander Hewitt became Deere & Company's fifth chairman.

But that was not this day.

This one happened sometime afterward. Hewitt could not even remember it exactly. He only recalled that it began with a piece of routine interoffice mail that arrived on his desk.

"It was a press release, from one of our competitors." Hewitt, a man of great warmth and near-regal bearing, but not at all intimidating, smiled slightly as he recounted the rest of the story.

"It announced some new product or other, nothing really of any threatening significance. But at the bottom of the sheet of paper was printed a kind of corporate slogan, a logo almost: "Not content to be runner-up."

"That's what it said," Hewitt remembered. "I think it was even in red ink.

"It started me thinking. Until that time, we had been content, even willing, to be runner-up. Always a steady, reliable, consistent number two behind International Harvester Company.

"And it made me wonder about being number one. What would it take? How long would it require? What kind of products did we need to introduce? What did we need to change? Was it anything more than just our own thinking, our own perception of Deere & Company?"

That was the day.

Not prepared to be second best, the current generation of Deere Company tractors leads the world's market. Running a 1990 castor-action mechanical front-wheel-drive assist Model 4455, Paul Eickert plows under old winter wheat at Brillion, Wisconsin. His Model 2810 four-bottom plow cuts 10 inches deep to prepare the soil for corn. The 4455 produced 128.8 drawbar and 142.7 PTO horsepower at 2200 rpm from six turbocharged cylinders with 4.57x4.75-inch bore and stroke.

While Joe Dain tested his all-wheel-drive tractor, shown above, the board asked him to look into motor cultivators. In September 1916, his first prototype Tractivator single-row cultivator was created.

CHAPTER 1

Early Experimental Tractors
The Reluctant Giant Awakes

When the Board of Directors of Deere & Company agreed in early 1912 to produce a tractor, it succumbed to internal and external pressures. These had been apparent to Deere's competitors for years. By 1912, International Harvester and J. I. Case were joined by nearly 200 other firms in the manufacture of self-propelled farm tractors. Deere's own branch managers had appealed to the board long before to recognize the farmers'—their customers'—growing interests. The managers saw sales following the tractors out of their doors, down the road, and into their competitors' retail outlets. Deere, producers of plows and crop seeding and harvesting equipment, still made products meant for use behind horses, mules, or oxen. These tools could be modified—by the farmer—for use behind a tractor.

In Atlanta and St. Louis, Deere branch managers incorporated into their own sales catalogs a large, 30-horsepower machine from Minneapolis, the Gas Traction Company's Big Four 30. This tractor was typical of the more powerful gasoline engine machines of the time. It weighed nearly 10 tons and was driven by steel rear wheels that were 8 feet tall. It had pulled a 7-bottom 14-inch Deere gangplow to win a gold medal at Winnipeg, Manitoba, Canada, in trials in 1910. The branch managers sought to capitalize on the Big Four's performance.

Within two years, Twin City tractors were appearing in Deere & Company brochures. The Model 40 tractor was shown demonstrating a 10-bottom gang in catalogs destined for export to South America.

Reluctantly, the board accepted what seemed inevitable. After nearly a decade of looking cautiously at the future of the self-propelled traction engine, whether steam or gasoline powered, board members stepped ahead—cautiously. On the first of July 1912, Staff Engineer C. H. Melvin was assigned to produce a tractor.

Resolved: That the preliminary work of designing an efficient small plow tractor be continued under the auspices of Mr. Dain and the Experimental Department.

—Deere & Co.
board minutes, 1914

Theo Brown, who had been superintendent of the Marseilles Company in East Moline, Illinois, since 1911 watched the development and later reported on Melvin's three-wheel tractor. Brown graduated in 1901 from Worcester Polytechnic Institute, Worcester, Massachusetts, and joined Deere in 1911. By 1916, he was head of the John Deere Plow Works Experimental Department, working closely with Chief Engineer Max Sklovsky.

Just before Brown retired in 1953, he summarized all of Deere & Company's earliest tractor development attempts in an internally published confidential report: "March 5, 1912, Deere & Co. Executive Committee resolved that 'A movement to produce a tractor plow should be started at once, having in view constantly, that the success of the same would be enhanced if not assured, were it possible to divorce the tractor from the plow and to thus make it available for general purposes.'"

Brown continued: "On July 1, 1912, Melvin was transferred from the Experimental Department at John Deere Plow Works to the General Company and given the assignment of designing and building an experimental tractor plow. A room in the plow works was provided."

Melvin's three-wheeler underwent practical field tests from late 1912 through early 1914. Melvin had clearly based his concept and design on that of a competitor, Hackney Manufacturing Company of St. Paul, Minnesota. Hackney's Auto-Plow had power enough to pull three plows, which Hackney placed below the operator, between the axles. In its tricycle configuration, the Auto-Plow could be operated with either axle leading. When its two drive wheels were leading, it plowed. When its single steering wheel was leading, it was capable of pulling wagons with its drawbar. The Auto-Plow had two seats facing each other, set close together, with the controls and the steering wheel in between. The driver shifted from one seat to the other, straddling the controls and the steering wheel.

Melvin's tricycle was similar. The operator's position, however, was moved farther from the engine on his version. The farmer sat at the extreme rear end in plowing applications, or nearer the front in drawbar applications.

Melvin apparently never received part of the board's message regarding making the plows removable. On his experiment, the plow could not be removed. However, one benefit accrued from this error. Melvin perfected a power lift mechanism for the plows that appeared again and again in later experiments and was eventually incorporated into production machines.

Brown recorded that around $6,800 was spent developing and testing Melvin's three-wheeler. But only one example was built, and by 1953, no test records remained in existence. Perhaps this was because the project was a failure: It was neither reliable nor strong enough to meet expectations.

Yet the Melvin experiment was far from the end of tractors at Deere. In fact, it was barely the beginning.

Joseph Dain Sr. joined Deere & Company as a board member when his own company—Dain Manufacturing Company in Ottumwa, Iowa—was acquired. Dain was something of a tinkerer who had begun producing agricultural implements from the background of being a successful furniture manufacturer. He produced hay-harvesting and -handling tools, and his company, although allied with Deere, was vigorously pursued by International Harvester in late 1903. Initially, International Harvester sought licensing agreements; then, it looked at outright purchase.

This was during a period when founder John Deere's son Charles ran Deere & Company. Charles was rapidly securing his own long-term marketing agreements, and in some cases even acquiring many of his former outside suppliers in an effort to thwart International Harvester's ambitions. After Charles' death in late October 1907, his successor, William Butterworth, further consolidated the company's far-flung agreements.

When Dain joined the Deere & Company folds on the last day of October 1910, he was rewarded with a vice presidency as well as his asking price. His position on the board and his interest in machines encouraged him to observe and react to the farmers' and the company's interest in tractors. His conclusions on Melvin's attempt were quoted in Brown's 1953 summary: "Joe Dain recalls it was a failure. Field performance—and trouble keeping it from breaking down—were problems."

"In 1914," Brown concluded, "development was stopped on the Melvin. The transition from heavy tractors moving slowly and pulling twelve or sixteen plows was giving way to smaller tractors which could pull three. Melvin had attempted to fit three plows underneath his tractor, like the Hackney Motor Plow [sic] which Leslie Hackney had applied for patent in 1910. Neither was a great success."

Deere & Company was still nervous about tractors. However, the board realized that the machines were a necessary evil. It was to Dain that the board turned next. Minutes of a meeting on May 27, 1914, told all: "Mr. Dain was asked to report to the Executive Committee whether or not a tractor could be built to sell at about $700 and in the meantime to suspend work of development until his report is made."

Days later, more minutes referred to the planned tractor offering: "June 9, 1914: Mr. Dain said he was working on a plan which he would submit as soon as completed. It was Mr. [Charles C.] Webber's idea that we should decide very soon whether or not a light tractor could be built to sell to the farmer for about $700. Mr. Dain further stated that the tractor he is planning would operate a three-bottom plow."

Charles C. Webber was another Deere & Company vice president and board member. He was the former owner of another subsidiary, Deere & Webber. He was also a grandson of John Deere.

A fortnight later a decision from the board came: "June 24, 1914: Resolved: That the preliminary work of designing an efficient small plow tractor be continued under the auspices of Mr. Dain and the Experimental Department."

Just after Labor Day, Dain reported to the board on his progress: "September 8, 1914: Mr. Dain reported that (more than) $6,000 had been expended in connection with work done by Mr. Melvin and further stated he thought he could build a light tractor for experimental purposes for about $3,000.00. Approved."

Dain worked through the winter, adapting ideas from other makers, including some from his predecessor, Melvin. Dain's new prototype was a tricycle, fitted with a four-cylinder Waukesha engine. However, unlike Melvin's tractor, with two wheels taking the power, Dain's—through driveshafts and chains—had power to all three. His two front wheels straddled the engine and also steered the tractor, and the single, center-mounted rear wheel supported implement weight as well as transferred engine traction to the ground.

In late winter 1915, Dain appeared before the board to report his progress. Caution and skepticism met his presentation, as recorded in the minutes: "February 13, 1915: Mr. Dain has developed a small experimental tractor and it is questionable whether we should enter into the manufacture of this machine."

Butterworth and some of the others did not hesitate to express their concerns. Deere & Company was not a tractor maker, and becoming one would require a huge investment. However, other considerations prevailed. Branch managers reported ever-increasing customer interest.

> "The question to be decided in the end was whether this machine or any little engine is going to be an economical thing for the farmer to buy. That we do not know as yet."
>
> —Charles Webber

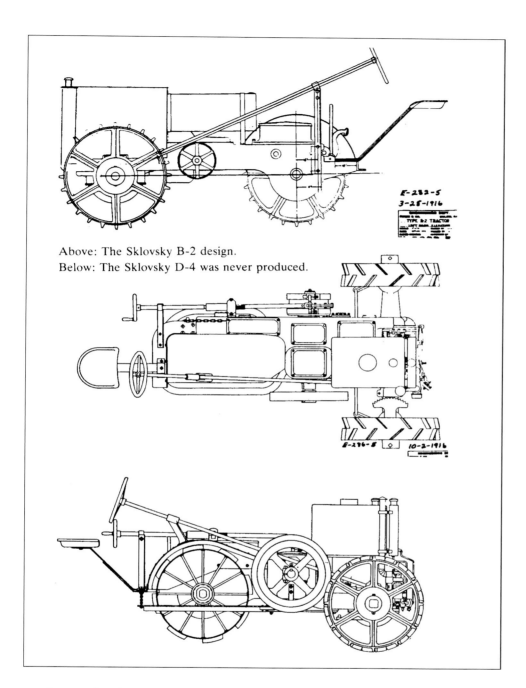

Above: The Sklovsky B-2 design.
Below: The Sklovsky D-4 was never produced.

While Deere's Board of Directors encouraged Joe Dain to develop his ideas into a profitable production tractor, the Board also assigned Max Sklovsky, head of the Design Department, to prepare another one, the B-2. Sklovsky's three-wheel B-2 prototype would not steer—its two-wheeled front axle was meant to steer but the axles had no differential.

these concerns, first to himself in personal memos and then to other board members during meetings inside the paneled rooms. His own inclinations were to follow faithfully the paths first described by his predecessor, Charles Deere: Proceed slowly, consolidate the company's holdings, and convert assets to cash whenever possible.

When Dain's tractor came up at an executive committee meeting in March, Butterworth's cautions were apparent. But once again, he did not prevail. Again, Brown quoted the minutes: "March 9, 1915: It was the sentiment of the Board:

"—That Mr. Dain should continue his work in connection with the tractor, give it a thorough trial in the field and continue its development;

"—That the present was not the time for Deere & Co. to decide whether it should go into the tractor business or not;

"—That it might seem wise later and it might not;

"—That the wise thing for the company to do was to watch the development of this business, and also to watch and develop the tractor, in order that the Company might be ready for any emergency."

The committee minutes concluded with one further piece of information: Up to that date, Dain had spent just about $2,890 on his experimental tractor. He was right on target.

During the six weeks following March 9, 1915, William Butterworth followed his path of caution. He had vigorously assured Deere & Company's bankers that the company was not in the business of making tractors and that it was not going into that business. How would those bankers—and other investors—react when they learned he had authorized further investment in tractor "experiments"?

But the pressure on Butterworth was great. His own board was made up largely of vice presidents who had formerly been presidents

"Now, Therefore, Be It Resolved," the February 13 minutes continued, "That Mr. Dain continue his work with the tractor now built until he considers it perfected, and that it be ascertained at that time the amount we have invested, for the purpose of fixing a basis upon which we would sell the same to a separate company for its development and sale. Also, that Mr. Dain advise the basis upon which his transmission can be used in said tractor."

While Dain continued to work on his prototype tractor in Deere's Experimental Department away from the mahogany-walled executive offices, Butterworth reconsidered his concerns. He wrote of of their own firms. These firms had been independent outside contractors and suppliers to Deere & Company. They had been successful enough to maintain long relationships with Deere & Company, relationships that went back to Charles Deere himself. These were businesses so successful that Deere & Company—under Charles and Butterworth himself—had acquired them. The men who previously ran them and now sat with Butterworth on the board were accustomed to reacting quickly to market pressures; their stake in their companies had been large, and their success had been measured in their own lifetime.

Butterworth had been appointed the second caretaker of a company grown vast beyond its founder's imagination. And he saw himself as caretaker much more than as innovator. Men with less at stake in this company were suggesting moves more rash than he would have wanted.

Did these men have a better feel for the future of the agricultural implement business? Perhaps they already had made their fortune, achieved in Deere & Company buy-outs of their own firms. Perhaps now these men felt they had nothing to lose. Daring moves, risky measures, were something outside Butterworth's repertoire of acceptable actions.

Butterworth had to consider Charles Webber, Minneapolis branch manager of Deere & Webber. In 1893, Webber had pressed Deere & Company to sell bicycles. Wayne G. Broehl Jr., author of *John Deere's Company*, quoted a memo from Webber to the board: "If there is anything in this bicycle business, any money to be made, we want to take hold of it."

There was money to be made. In 1895, Deere & Company listed $150,000 in sales from bicycles alone. Races were staged, and thousands of bicycles were sold—including, by 1896, John Deere's own private label bike. Yet, bicycles faded from public interest and from the sales summaries in 1897.

Butterworth also had to consider Joseph Dain of Dain Manufacturing, now wholly absorbed within the benevolent parentage of Deere & Company. Dain was known as an independent, self-sufficient businessman. Webber acknowledged that reputation to Dain in a letter, also quoted in *John Deere's Company*: "We have heard it rumored that your Company was negotiating for the sale of their plant to the International Harvester Co . . . . Now I don't know whether there is anything in it or not, but should rather think not, as I have always thought that you were the kind of fellow that wanted to run your own business pretty much your own way."

To Butterworth, the questions concerning tractors must have triggered his worst imaginings. Bicycles were one thing. At first, Deere had only marketed bikes manufactured by others; then, it simply rebadged outside products. But tractors were different. Dain was proposing that Deere develop and produce its own tractors, and doing so required expensive machine tooling.

Was Dain operating his tractor experiment within Deere as an independent spirit? Or worse, was he an independent businessman now bankrolled by the company's backers?

Tractors were a new product line to Deere. Tractor development had undone other formerly strong competitors, such as Rumely and Hart-Paar. The conditions affecting agriculture were so mercurial that fortunes had been lost in a single bad season. Bad weather followed by bad weather could doom a manufacturer that had sold products on credit.

Yet, Webber and Dain watched International Harvester and J. I. Case, and they could sense what might happen if Deere & Company—that is, Butterworth—did not accede and accept the challenge to develop a tractor line.

On May 9, 1915, Webber reported to the executive committee that Dain was planning to revise his next tractor and make some improvements. Webber recommended keeping the tractor at work to determine its weaknesses. He suggested sending the new version to a different test site—Minneapolis, his former branch—where it could plow 300 or 400 acres and get a thorough workout. Whereupon Ralph Lourie, manager of the John Deere Plow Company at Moline, Illinois, suggested that it might be better still if at least five tractors were out testing in a variety of conditions.

Butterworth prepared to speak again. But Lourie had anticipated Butterworth's worries. Lourie had an idea. Would it be possible to start a new business, outside Deere & Company, to sell the tractors? Would that relieve Deere & Company of any responsibilities?

Lourie pointed out that the branch managers were reporting that some sales of plows had been lost because of tractors. Deere Company made plows only for horse or mule teams. These plows had wheels, and they could not be adapted to some tractors—like Deere's very own Melvin—where the plows fitted beneath the machine. Lourie reminded the board of its vulnerability to competitors that sold tractors as well as plows.

Webber told Butterworth it was important for the bankers to understand what this new tractor was. Theo Brown quoted the board minutes paraphrasing Webber's arguments: "The bankers had very good reasons to be scared about gas tractors but they had in mind the Rumely, the Emerson and the Hart-Paar people. They have made a heavy, clumsy machine and have made a failure, and have not made any money. They [the bankers] think it is something we are going to sell on two or three years time [payments], while we are talking about something that is entirely different.

"The question to be decided in the end," Webber concluded, "was whether this machine or any little engine is going to be an economical thing for the farmer to buy. That we do not know as yet."

Webber rested his case like a trial lawyer appealing the death sentence contemplated for a client. The jury voted in his favor: "Resolved: That without attempting to at this time define our final policy toward the tractor business further than the resolution passed at the Directors' meeting held February 13, 1915, but with a view of trying out more thoroughly the Dain tractor, Mr. [George W.] Mixter be requested to cooperate with Mr. Dain in order to hasten the try-out of the present machine and to determine upon the improvements that should be made in it, with the authority to build from three to six of the revised experimental tractors to be thoroughly tried out this Summer and Fall."

Mixter, a board member, was vice president in charge of manufacturing. He was also John Deere's great-grandson. He had steadily supported Butterworth throughout the year, but on this matter, he counseled his older relative to reconsider. In a letter to Butterworth, unearthed by Wayne Broehl, he stated his case: "The county is now flooded with attempts at practical small tractors, and the extremely wide desire of the farmers to buy such a small tractor cannot be entirely overlooked. . . . If it be possible to build a small tractor that will really stand up for five or more years' work on the farm, I believe they will be a permanent requirement of the American farmer and"—Mixter delivered his point economically—"especially in view of the plow trade they carry with them, this possibility cannot be overlooked by Deere & Company."

Throughout the summer and fall, Mixter worked with Dain, testing and developing his three prototypes. Just before Christmas, Dain himself reported his most recent results to the board.

His first tractor weighed nearly 3,800 pounds and used his innovative friction-drive transmission, which allowed the operator to shift gears on the fly, from low to high speed, without stopping. This transmission incorporated a double clutch, with faces on both sides. Each clutch had an inner and an outer shaft, allowing both sets of gears to be constantly in mesh as engaging one clutch disengaged the other. In a shop test on a kind of chassis dynamometer, Dain produced a steady 5,000-pound drawbar pull in low gear. In the spring of 1916, this proved to be more than 3,000 pounds in the actual field tests.

From the final drive, chains drove the axles. Dain had earlier reported that the first chains were not strong enough and broke. A heavier-gauge chain replaced them and cured the problem. Two front ratchets had broken and were replaced with parts made from heavier metal. Engine overheating problems were solved in the subsequent prototypes by using a larger Long Manufacturing Company radiator and a larger fan. (Perfex radiators from Racine, Wisconsin, appeared on the production models.) The rear-wheel-drive gears showed considerable wear, but this convinced Dain all the more of the wisdom of his all-wheel drive; splitting the traction had saved the rear end from likely destruction.

The second tractor weighed nearly 4,000 pounds and, at Webber's direction, was sent for testing to Winnebago in south central Minnesota. There, the first economic figures were developed.

"It plowed eighty acres," Dain reported, "at a cost of fifty-nine cents per acre, counting the man's time at thirty cents an hour. The soil here was of heavy black gumbo and was in poor condition owing to the almost continual rain—several days [that] we plowed, the neighboring farmers thought it too wet to plow with their horses. We pulled three fourteen-inch bottoms six inches deep at two-and-a-half miles per hour." This was the same kind of soil that had made John Deere's reputation 78 years earlier.

The third prototype was completed just before the March board meeting. The transmission was modified, replacing the worm-and-gear

and internal gear drive with a chain drive to the rear wheel. Dain took the new machine to Deere's Laredo, Texas, test farm for evaluation, and followed up with a telegram to Mixter, reproduced in Brown's book:

San Antonio, Tex. March 13, 1916
Deere & Company
Moline, Ill.

Have followed tractor closely for two weeks. Conditions extremely hard and rough. Absolutely no weakness in construction. Gears, chains, universals, in fact all parts in good condition. Tractor has travelled near five hundred miles under extreme load. Change speed gear a wonder. I recommend to the Board that we build ten machines at once.

Joseph Dain

It is not difficult to imagine what it must have sounded like inside the board room when Mixter read this telegram on March 14, 1916. Mixter then added his own observations. He explained that Dain's previous friction-type transmission had been discontinued. The new transmission, the gear type, still had a few bugs, but they could be worked out quickly to get the tractor to manufacture. And Mixter believed that Deere & Company could manufacture the tractor in already existing factory space, spending not more than $50,000 on patterns, jigs, new tools, and machinery.

If Butterworth ever felt the carpet slipping from beneath his feet, it may have been at that moment.

The March 14 minutes read: "Whereas, Mr. Joseph Dain has developed several small tractors which have been experimentally tried out, the latest machine proving successful in Texas for a sufficient time to demonstrate its practicability from a general standpoint and,

"Whereas, It is desirable that this machine should now be reconstructed to meet such minor questions as have developed in Texas for a sufficient time to demonstrate its practicability from a general standpoint, and

"Whereas, It is desirable that this machine should now be reconstructed to meet such minor questions as have developed in Texas, and to make it suitable for economical manufacturing and then turned over to a manufacturing organization,

"Resolved, That Mr. Dain be requested to reconstruct said tractor with such modifications as may be deemed wise by him and his associates, preparatory to economical manufacturing;

"Further, That the Marseilles Plant (now the John Deere Spreader Works) be directed to take up this tractor work with the object of getting it on a manufacturing basis as a possible part of their regular line;

"Further, That about ten machines be built by the Marseilles Company, at the earliest practical date;

"Further, That both Mr. Dain and the Marseilles Company be directed to vigorously continue tractor development work."

On March 14, 1916, Deere & Company stepped into the farm tractor business.

Deere & Company Board member and Vice President Joe Dain was given his assignment in March 1916: "Mr. Dain [will] reconstruct said tractor with such modifications as may be deemed wise by him and his associates, preparatory to economical manufacturing." Deere's goal was a salable $700 tractor. It got more: four cylinders and all wheel-drive, strength, and reliability to sell for $1,200.

CHAPTER 2

Dain All-Wheel Drive
Deere's First Production Tractor

By mid-June 1916, Theo Brown's Marseilles Company had begun the manufacture of the next five Joe Dain development tractors. An additional machine was being assembled at Moline. The gear-transmission prototype was shipped up from Texas to Minot, North Dakota, where everyone seemed pleased with its continuing performance.

A question of engines arose. Dain explained the difficulties he had experienced in testing various powerplants available on the market. These troubles were related as much to their service and the inaccessibility of parts for removal and replacement as to their general reliability. Walter McVicker had been enlisted to help, and he had begun to design a new engine.

McVicker had been a mechanical engineer with the Alma Manufacturing Company in Alma, Michigan. During his four years with that well-regarded gasoline engine maker, he also developed and introduced a novel four-cycle gasoline engine, the McVicker Automatic. This used a separate chamber alongside the piston cylinder, pressurized by the engine compression, to push open the exhaust valve, doing away with the exhaust valve pushrods.

In 1908, McVicker left Alma to open his own firm, McVicker Engineering Company in Minneapolis. A year later, he entered a partnership with Mack Joy to develop and produce the Joy-McVicker tractor, which was produced by Alma Manufacturing. It was, however, his engineering company to which Dain turned for help.

Based on specifications Dain and George W. Mixter provided, McVicker began designing a new engine specifically for Deere & Company's tractor in the middle of June 1916. Dain reported to the

"We firmly believe the machine, generally, is perfected to a point where it can be successfully manufactured commercially, and we strongly recommend you proceed with the construction of at least 100 as soon as possible."

—George Schutz

executive committee that McVicker's first prototypes were expected in the fall. Meanwhile, Waukesha engines would be fitted to the six new tractor prototypes to be shipped out for testing in August.

On July 13, Mixter sent the board a memo that fulfilled another requirement of the earlier resolution. "Original cost figures," he wrote, "were $736 (for 1.25 in steel)—$761 (2.25-inch steel). These figures are based on paying $200 for the motor. The writer . . . believes that the machine as today designed with the motor figured at $200 can be built for $600 (1.25[-inch] steel) cost of manufacture.

"This means," Mixter added, "judged in light of other goods of our manufacture that the farmer should pay $1,200 for the machine. This is somewhat higher than had been considered admissible for a three-plow tractor. It is the writer's belief however," he concluded, "that an all-wheel drive will ultimately be the tractor the farmer will pay for."

Three Dain development models were testing in Minnesota by mid-September, another remained in Minot, still another had been shipped to Huron, South Dakota, and the sixth had only just been sent to Fargo, North Dakota.

Almost two months later, Dain again reported progress to the board. Working out of the Deere & Webber Minneapolis branch, testers noted some trouble with the clutch collar and bevel pinion sleeve, and they questioned various aspects of the engine itself and its belt power. But on the whole, their report read much like a paid product endorsement.

"The all-wheel drive makes its light weight possible," wrote George P. Schutz, branch manager of Deere & Webber, "and gives the

maximum traction, the advantages of which are that the tractor will go through more difficult conditions without miring down than any other tractor, and in the event it does mire down, by uncoupling the plows, it will always pull itself out, which other tractors cannot do," Schutz and a territory salesman, John Molstad, also noticed that the tractor's light weight did not compact the soil so much as the competition's tractors did.

The new Deere tractor's ostensibly complex drivetrain in fact provided benefits. "Four chains being used to drive the wheels," Schutz continued, "divides the strain on the sprockets and chains, making the chain drive, in our judgement, two or three times more durable than gears and much easier for the farmer to replace and adjust.

"Another big advantage of this feature," Schutz concluded, "is that there is no noise. The noise made by the gears and the exhaust, on many tractors, especially after they have been used for some little time, is almost unbearable."

Schutz's report also incorporated a kind of marketing survey that he and Molstad accomplished while visiting farmers throughout Minnesota and North and South Dakota. Schutz felt the farmers'

comments were well worth considering as Deere & Company got closer to starting regular production.

"A tractor, like a man or horse, cannot work to its limit continuously and last," one older "philosopher" observed. In Aberdeen, South Dakota, Schutz and Molstad found a witness to that philosophy in a man who used a six-plow-rated tractor to pull four plows. "He stated," Schutz recorded, "that he wore out one tractor in a short time by pulling all he could with it, and he made up his mind that the only way a tractor would stand up was for it to have enough power so it would 'play' with the plow, so to speak."

Meanwhile, a Fargo implement dealer exposed a pitfall to Schutz and Molstad. "He stated that if a customer has trouble—and they all seem to have an undue amount—he will blame the Fargo Implement Co. just the same, and when the farmer is ready to buy a gang plow the probabilities are he will go to their competitor and get it."

The same dealer had sold 17 Waterloo tractors in the past two years. He suggested he could have sold 17 more but was reluctant; if he had, his repair staff would have been overwhelmed, occupied full-time looking after the troublesome tractors. Yet, he also sold 17 Deere & Company Pony Plows, one for each tractor. Without the tractor, he suspected he probably would have sold only a quarter as many plows.

Schutz listened carefully, and thoroughly understood what he heard. His recommendations spoke with insight. "This goes to show," he wrote, "that our dealers need a tractor badly but that they must have a good one. . . . Our tractor should be strong enough and have power enough to pull three bottoms in stubble, under almost any condition, as the majority of farmers when purchasing a three-plow tractor expect it to be able to do better and deeper plowing than they could with horses. In fact, a good many tractors are sold at times when plowing conditions are unusually hard for horses.

"We think," Schutz continued, "the matter of price should be forgotten for the present. Go ahead and build the tractor—first class all the way through, using extra good magnetos, carburetors, etc., as well as making it extra good in other details. And when that is done, if the price must of necessity be $1,500 to market them profitably, let's sell them for that."

He went on to question, though, whether the new tractor really needed to be so costly when competitors' tractors of greater weight were retailing for less. His arguments offered unconvincing statistics and never took into account that Deere's new tractor was all-wheel driven. However, his point was yet to come.

"In considering the matter of price we must remember the more tractors we sell the more tractor plows we will sell!"

Schutz signed his name with a flourish reminiscent of John Hancock's signature on the Declaration of Independence. Yet, William Butterworth was still mired in the gumbo of caution.

Rumors suggested that a tractor capable of pulling more than just three plows should be investigated, and that a motor cultivator should be planned as well.

George Peek, a protégé of Charles Webber who had gone on to manage Deere & Company's Omaha branch, was named to the executive committee soon after that promotion in 1916. He wrote to Butterworth as a committee member advising continued development and encouraging the expansion of tractor manufacture.

Butterworth, who needed to miss the mid-September board meeting, wrote back to Peek and forced upon him the chair's proxy. Wayne Broehl quoted Butterworth's confidential letter: "I have acquiesced," Butterworth began, "in the experimental work which has been done, but I am beginning to feel that we are wasting the stockholders' money in going any further with it. . . . Ford's active interest in the tractor business means unlimited capital and resources for marketing. . . . I want it plainly understood that I am and will remain opposed to our taking up the manufacture of tractors and will take steps to stop it if an attempt is made to start. . . . If it comes up, I want you to stop it."

Whereas Butterworth saw Ford as a considerable threat to be avoided, Peek and the others saw Ford—and International Harvester—as competition that should no longer be avoided.

After Schutz's encouraging report was read out loud to the board, Butterworth learned a painful lesson: Never miss a board meeting. The minutes recorded the board's action: "September 12, 1917: Resolved, that Mr. Dain be authorized to continue his negotiations with the thought in mind of buying not over 100 of the Dain tractors outside with the view of continuing the development on the tractor line, the purchase to be made on a fixed price basis."

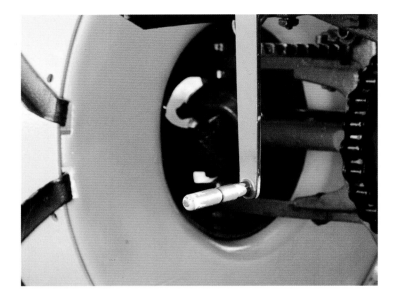

Top: From Dain's final drive, chains drove the axles. The first efforts revealed inadequate chain strength—they simply broke. Replaced with heavier-gauge chain, they wore evenly and slowly. Front ratchets—universals—also failed. These were remanufactured from heavier metal.

Bottom: Shop tests on an early chassis dynamometer produced a steady 5,000-pound drawbar pull in low gear. In the spring of 1916, Dain pulled more than 3,000 pounds in actual field tests. The prototype tractor itself weighed 3,800 pounds. The traction of the All-Wheel Drive contributed to its strength and durability.

This "outside" supplier was to be none other than Deere Company's Marseilles works in East Moline, where the company's first binders had been built, and where Dain's development tractors had already been assembled.

On October 24, Dain traveled with Schutz to Huron to watch three of his prototypes. In 1916, Deere & Webber had loaned to its agent, F. R. Brumwell—who owned three ranches—one of the Dain prototypes fitted with the Waukesha engine. After a year of use, Deere had overhauled the tractor and replaced the original Waukesha engine with the new McVicker powerplant and returned it to the agent. Schutz and Dain watched Brumwell's son, Roy, plow several rounds of his field with a three-furrow Pony Plow set first at a 6–7-inch depth and then, as a great challenge, at an 8–10-inch depth. Plowing in heavy black loam, the prototype exhibited no undue wheel slippage and no engine knock. The senior Brumwell had been impressed enough with the tractor that he bought three, each with the new McVicker engine. One the agent kept, and the other two he sold to customers—possibly the first sales ever of John Deere tractors.

In visiting other test sites, Schutz and Dain concluded once and for all that the early Waukesha engines had inadequate power for the kind of work a three-plow-rated tractor was expected to do. The 1917 versions of the Dain tractor with the new four-cylinder McVicker were more powerful, and the drivetrain problems—having to do with clutch thrust and bevel pinion shaft bearings—were eliminated through a redesign using ball and roller bearings. Heavier drive chains eliminated the breakage problems. The new gear transmission ran submerged in oil, guaranteeing cooler running and better lubrication.

Servicing had been a significant element in McVicker's design for the new engine. It allowed a major engine overhaul—removal of the cylinder head, even pistons and connecting rods—without a complete engine teardown. Transmission service could be accomplished by merely removing a cover plate.

"Finally," Schutz wrote, in concluding his report of the trip with Dain, "we firmly believe the machine, generally, is perfected to a point where it can be successfully manufactured commercially, and we strongly recommend you proceed with the construction of at least 100 as soon as possible."

Schutz's report was quickly approved by executive committee members Charles Velie, Charles Webber, and Floyd Todd and was forwarded to the entire executive committee.

Sadly, Dain never lived to see even a seventh John Deere tractor built. Overworked and overtired before his trip to South Dakota began, he contracted pneumonia during the two-day visit. On October 31, 1917, he died in a hospital in Minneapolis.

In his 1953 summary, Brown quoted the minutes from the executive committee meeting held on November 19, 1917: "Resolved, That Mr. [Leon] Clausen be requested to proceed with the manufacture of 100 tractors of the Dain type using for that purpose such members of the organization as are available and such outside assistance as it is advisable to obtain, provided, however, that the personnel of the organization called into this branch of the business shall be decided upon after confer-

Prototypes used a four-cylinder Waukesha engine but the production All-Wheel Drive tractors used a specially designed McVicker four. With 4.50x5.00-inch bore and stroke, the cast-in-bloc, detachable-head engine produced 12 horsepower at the drawbar, 24 on the belt pulley. Production tractors produced in 1918 and 1919 weighed 4,600 pounds.

ence with the Executive Committee and that the Executive Committee and the Conference Committee as well be fully advised and conferred with from time to time during the progress of the work, and

"Further, It is the opinion of those present that the services of Joseph Dain Jr., who has had wide experience in the development of the tractor in connection with the work of his father, should be made use of to the fullest extent and in as important a capacity as his experience and abilities permit."

Clausen had been, until 1916, manager of Dain's former hay tool works in Ottumwa. At that time, he was transferred to Moline to fill in as head of manufacturing while Lieutenant Colonel Mixter fulfilled his army obligations.

The man next named responsible for the manufacture of the new John Deere All-Wheel Drive tractors was Elmer McCormick, superintendent at Deere's Tenth Street factory in East Moline—the former Root & Van Dervoort engine shops, which Deere leased for its binder works. McCormick had worked closely with Dain almost from the start while studying engineering at the University of Illinois and had contributed in minor ways to the design and engineering of the All-Wheel Drive.

Other departments were brought in at this point. A duotone sales brochure was produced. The cover showed Dain's All-Wheel Drive tractor pulling a three-bottom plow away from the camera under the heading "The John Deere All-Wheel Drive Tractor." The single-sheet promotional piece, folded in half and in half again to standard letter size, opened up to reveal a full side-profile photograph and six smaller

engineering detail photos. Specifications covered the back page.

An *Instruction Book and Repair List for the John Deere Tractor* was also produced, dated July 1918. It could not be mistaken as a manual for any kind of later-production tractor; on page 12, under the general heading "Motor" and subheading "Piston Assembly," the parts list called for four gray-iron pistons, part number TM207. Likewise, it required four steel connecting rods and caps, part number TM5002.

On December 11, 1917, Clausen reported back to the executive committee. Manufacture was set to begin on the 100 tractors. Contracts for the McVicker engines had been let. Clausen expected that the first half of the planned production would be completed and ready for shipment by June 1, 1918.

As Deere & Company geared up production for its new 4,600-pound steel tractor, its need for a major tractor manufacturing facility became clear. Deere had already investigated other manufacturing installations in the Midwest and was aware of the Waterloo Gasoline Engine Company, some 110 miles northwest of Moline in Waterloo, Iowa. Most appealing to Deere & Company was an acquisition the gas engine company had made: in October 1912, it had bought the Waterloo Foundry.

On March 14, 1918, Deere & Company would invest in Waterloo. The $2.35 million purchase price, unanimously approved by the board, would include the Waterloo Gasoline Engine Company, inheritor of the Waterloo Foundry's 8–15 Big Chief Tractor—predecessor of the Waterloo Boy Model L.

Wanting adequate space to manufacture its own tractor, Deere & Company
looked at the Waterloo Gasoline Engine Company, an established maker
with its own foundry. Waterloo began producing tractors called the
Waterloo Boy in 1912 and continued with subtle modifications and
improvements through this 1915 Model R Style D and beyond.

CHAPTER 3

The Waterloo Boy
One Giant Step—In Place

Like any better-than-average industrial project, John Deere's All-Wheel Drive tractor was conceived, developed, tested, and produced in utter secrecy. Not only the firm's competition, but even its bankers, should not know about it.

President William Butterworth had on his hands a clearly superior product, full of technical innovation. It appeared, after thorough farm field testing, to be reliable, strong, and a good value for the money, even at the $1,650 asking price quoted by the Huron branch office, the F. R. Brumwell agency.

Six weeks after an executive committee resolution to go ahead with production, Joseph Dain Sr. was dead. Three weeks after his death, the board proclaimed Dain's tractor alive and gave full authorization to begin regular production with 100 machines. This was probably a compromise figure, likely settled upon to keep Butterworth from going through the ceiling and to keep his bankers from going through the door.

All of which provoked young Willard Lamb Velie. Velie was the youngest son of Stephen H. Velie, John Deere's son-in-law. (Stephen Velie joined Deere in 1863, three years after his marriage to Emma Deere. A successful businessman on his own, he became the Deere and Company secretary and a personal friend to his brother-in-law, Charles Deere.) When Stephen died 1895, Willard, his youngest son, assumed both his job as Deere & Company secretary and his seat on the board. Even when Willard left the company to operate Velie Carriage Company in 1900, he remained on the board. Velie Carriage evolved into Velie Engineering Company, which metamorphosed into Velie Motors Corporation. By 1916, was producing the Velie Biltwell 12–24, a four-cylinder farm tractor. The Biltwell weighed

around 4,500 pounds and sold for about $1,750. It was not all-wheel drive.

It was from this position as an outside competitor that Velie appeared again to haunt the board.

Wayne Broehl chronicled the written confrontation, which consisted of a letter from Velie to Butterworth and the board. Velie reminded the board of its unanimous resolution from March 5, 1912, "to produce a tractor plow . . . at once." He reminded it that nearly six years had passed, 12 tractors had been built, $250,000 had been spent, and the company position had deteriorated against that of its competition because of its unwillingness to move ahead.

Velie was outspoken. He forcefully presented his conclusions, which he aimed directly at the status quo: "We cannot profitably make as small a number as 100 tractors, [because] in the process [of doing so] we become competitors of the independent tractor manufacturers, who have been heretofore our 'allies.' . . . I cannot refrain," he stressed, "from remarking that we should build tractors largely and whole-heartedly, or dismiss the tractor matter as inconsequential and immaterial."

It was near the end of January 1918. On the 25th, during a board meeting, Velie's letter to Butterworth was read into the minutes. It had the effect of a fox let loose in a chicken coop.

The manager of the company's harvester works, W. R. Morgan, had recently come from International Harvester. He expressed strong concern over the effect that newcomer Henry Ford would have on any tractor market once his machines were in the marketplace. But having heard the evidence of customer demand and growing

> *"I cannot refrain from remarking that we should build tractors largely and wholeheartedly, or dismiss the tractor matter as inconsequential and immaterial."*
>
> —Willard Velie

23

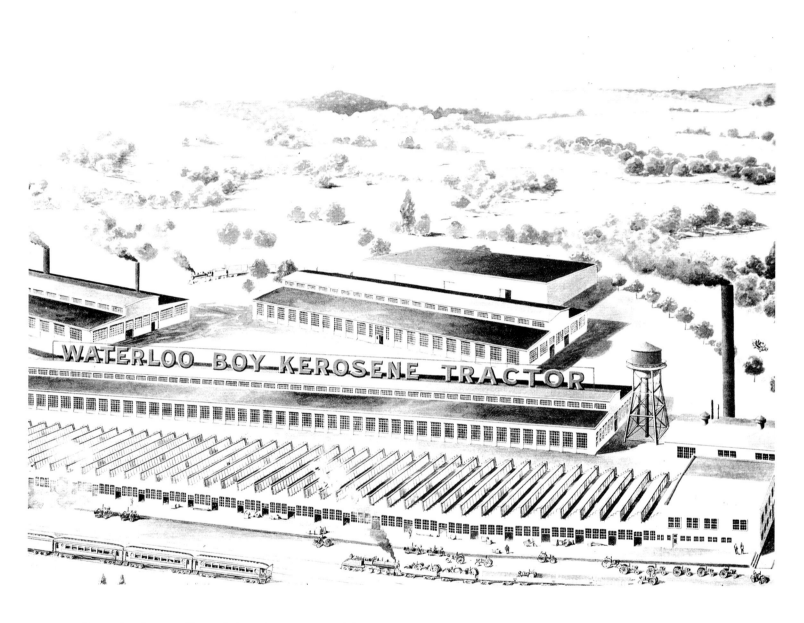

Above: In March 1918, Deere purchased the Waterloo Gasoline Tractor Company, its tractors, patents, and works for $2,350,000.

Opposite page: This 1915 Model R Style D, number 1,643, is one of the last Style D Model R tractors produced in the fall of 1915. The Style E that followed introduced the slightly larger engine, increasing bore 0.50 inch to 6.00 inches.

customer frustration because Deere did not have a tractor, Morgan voiced support for Velie's recommendation. "If it is coming, and I believe we cannot stop it, we should get into it some way."

Frank Silloway was acting head of sales. He was filling in for George Peek, who had joined George Mixter in the World War I effort. Silloway renewed an idea that had been introduced in earlier board meetings. With Deere & Company's limited tractor production capacity at that time and with the slow start-up that this insufficient capacity almost certainly guaranteed, might Deere & Company be better off buying an existing, established tractor maker?

The Waterloo Gasoline Engine Company, Silloway had heard, was available. Its president, George Miller, wanted to retire—with cash in the bank. Knowing little more than that—and that various

Deere branches had sold Waterloo Boy tractors with greater and lesser success—the board told Silloway to go forth and find the facts.

The facts were impressive. Silloway's investigations revealed a company producing two models: a single-speed Model R, which was introduced in 1914, and a newer, two-speed Model N, just introduced in 1917. Both tractors used a horizontally mounted

two-cylinder engine. Both ran on inexpensive kerosene. In 1918, the R sold for $985, and the N sold for $1,150.

Both tractors were rated at 12 horsepower from the drawbar, 25 horsepower from the belt pulley. However, the new N used roller bearings in the engine and had adopted automobile-type steering to replace the Model R's bolster-and-chain steering system. In addition, the Waterloo company marketed a line of stationary and portable engines, running on either gasoline or kerosene. Sales of all models had been good: 2,762 in 1916 and 4,007 in 1917.

The factory was large and well equipped, with many new machine and production tools. In addition to the buildings, the company owned an adjoining plot of 38 acres of vacant land to handle anticipated expansion. Finally, while producing its predecessor to the Model R, a tractor called the Waterloo Boy Model 15,

which had used a horizontally opposed two-cylinder engine, the company had acquired the Waterloo Foundry. As a tractor manufacturer, it was "vertically integrated"—that is, completely self-sufficient.

The Waterloo Gasoline Engine Company evolved from one of America's earliest experiments with gasoline engines. An itinerant thresherman, John Froehlich, had achieved some success working with a J. I. Case straw-burning steam traction engine and a threshing machine. With a large crew, he traveled through four harvest seasons, working in Iowa and South Dakota, beginning in 1888. Fascinated by gasoline power, he bought a very early Van Duzen engine and fitted it to a Robinson tractor chassis. After more than a year of effort, he had a working tractor completed in time for the harvest in 1892, and he gave it a 52-day shakedown trial in South Dakota.

Outside interest was sufficient and results were encouraging enough that Froehlich decided to go into full-scale production. He enlisted financial backing from Miller and several other Waterloo businessmen. Together, they founded the Waterloo Gasoline Traction Engine Company.

Between 1893 and 1896, Froehlich produced only four of his tractors. Two of these sold and were subsequently returned as failures. His partners encouraged him to continue at least the production of stationary and portable engines; these had worked, sold, and generated some profit. But Froehlich was single-minded in his devotion to tractors, and without support from his partners, he left his firm.

After Froehlich's departure, the partners reorganized the company as the Waterloo Gasoline Engine Company, remaining faithful to their own inclinations. Louis W. Witry, an engineer with Santa Fe Railroad in New Mexico, joined the firm and took over as engine designer and engineer. Within a few years, the company again became interested in tractors. Harry Leavitt, who had more successful experience in tractor design and engineering, was enlisted to experiment with crawler track adaptations. By 1913, the

Above: Style D and earlier Waterloo Boy Model R tractors fitted the fuel tank upright. But as the fuel reached the bottom of the tank, especially on downslopes, the carburetor starved and this forced a modification. The tank was laid horizontal and place on small stands. Then, in 1920, the stands were raised, eliminating the problem once and for all.

Opposite page: The earliest Waterloo Boy tractors used automobile-type steering. But most of the R and N series reverted to the bolster-and-chain— or aim-and-pray—steering system until January 1920. Large springs mounted on the front axles absorbed the shock of crossing furrows or other obstructions, but slack in the steering required plenty of advance thinking and vigorous cranking before coming to the fences.

Waterloo Gasoline Engine Company had introduced its Waterloo Boy One-Man Tractor, a relatively small tractor for the time, at 9,000 pounds.

The name Waterloo Boy had been introduced sometime in 1896 when the company first produced stationary engines to power water pumps, among other things. This name was likely meant to be a play on the term "water boy," which described the person who was needed to fetch and deliver water around the farm.

From Waterloo's One-Man Tractor clearly evolved the Waterloo Boy Models R and N that Silloway so much admired. Even though Deere's own tractor had four cylinders and all-wheel drive, Silloway seemed quite taken with Waterloo's machine. Witry's sales spiel justified its two cylinders and rear-wheel drive. Upon Silloway's return to Deere, he described the various "advantages" of two cylinders in a long memo, quoted in Broehl's *John Deere's Company*:

1st: A two cylinder tractor can be built cheaper than a four and price is an important factor, because the tractor is a business machine and must win by its economy.

2nd: The tractor, unlike the automobile, must pull hard all the time. The bearing must be adjusted for wear. There are half as many bearings to adjust on a two cylinder tractor and half as many valves to grind.

3rd: There are less parts to get out of order and cause delay.

4th: The bearings are more accessible on a two cylinder horizontal engine than a four cylinder vertical engine.

5th: Two cylinders will burn kerosene better than four.

6th: Four cylinders are not necessary on tractors. The fact that a tractor is geared 50 to 1 instead of 4 to 1 eliminates all jerky motion. The engine of a tractor can be made heavy and have a heavy flywheel and can be mounted on a strong rigid frame. Therefore, a two cylinder engine is satisfactory in a tractor and when it is, why go to the four cylinder type.

Silloway was convinced: "I believe that, quality and price considered, it [the Waterloo] is the best commercial tractor on the market today."

Silloway was enthused: "The Waterloo tractor is of a type which the average farmer can buy. . . . We should have a satisfactory tractor at a popular price, and not a high-priced tractor built for the few."

Silloway was evangelical: "Here we have an opportunity to, overnight, step into practically first place in the tractor business."

Management, still lightly mired in the gumbo, voted to sleep on it.

Silloway was their alarm clock.

When Miller telephoned on March 14, 1918, to advise Deere & Company's board that its option expired that day, Silloway became the board's magneto, initiating the motion to buy Waterloo so that Deere would not lose the opportunity to buy the established tractor manufacturing facility.

The vote was unanimous. Charles Webber, Charles Velie, Floyd Todd, even Butterworth and Joseph Dain Jr., voted to buy. Mixter and Peek were at war, and Willard Velie was absent.

In his 1953 book, Theo Brown theorized about what the Waterloo purchase meant and what options it presented for Deere's own tractor plans. After the first 100 All-Wheel Drives were produced, further manufacture was uncertain and no further development work was done. Production was completed in 1919, and all 100 were shipped to Brumwell in the Huron branch for sale.

"In 1918," Brown began, "most of the full line implement companies were building tractors, particularly International Harvester Company and Case. It was felt that it was imperative to get into the tractor business at as early a moment as possible in order for Deere & Co. to hold onto their plow business. A tractor and plow were usually sold by the same dealer.

"The Dain tractor," he went on, "while a good tractor, was high-priced . . . it would require considerable time to tool up for manufacture.

"Deere & Co. had purchased the Waterloo Gasoline Engine Co. and thus had a factory, a tractor and an organization that was functioning, and so [Deere] was in the tractor business at one quick stroke.

"In concluding," Brown wrote, "it should be emphasized that in his thinking about tractors, Mr. Dain was ahead of his time, for he insisted that tractors must be made better in every way, and that price was not the main objective. Many features of the Dain tractor were better than those of most tractors of that period."

In his own conclusions two weeks after the purchase, Velie wrote to Butterworth to try to reassure the still-hesitant Deere & Company president: "I am more than satisfied we have made the best move Deere & Company has ever made, and that it was an extremely fortunate thing we were able to buy this plant. I believe, if we handle this proposition right, the Waterloo Boy will be to the tractor trade what the Ford car is to the automobile trade. Of course the Ford tractor will take first place, but if we can take second place that will be good enough for us."

Left: Schebler carburetors were used and fuel ignition was sparked by a Dixie Model 44 magneto. The small glass globes showed proof that the lubricating oil was flowing through the engine. The cylinder head and block were cast in one piece on early Rs. Only 65 of these Style D Model R tractors were produced.

Opposite page: Model R tractors used Waterloo's horizontally mounted side-by-side twin-cylinder engines. With bore and stroke of 5.50x7.00 inches used on the Style A through Style D tractors, pulley horsepower was rated at 24. In mid-1915, engine displacement increased to a bore and stroke of 6.00x7.00 inches, yet rated output remained at 12 drawbar and 24 pulley horsepower.

The Overtime Farm Tractor Company was located in London's East End, just before the start of World War I. Selling for £325, the Overtime was, for all the world, Waterloo Gasoline Engine Company's export Model R or N. Manufacture and export of the Overtime tractors continued for nearly two years after Deere bought Waterloo.

CHAPTER 4

The English Overtime
Ford Meets His Waterloo

On March 30, 1918, while Charles Velie was sending his reassurances to William Butterworth in Moline, Henry Ford was producing 64 Fordson tractors in Detroit. Ford produced 64 tractors every day, and he had already shipped 7,000 to the United Kingdom. Charging cost plus $50, he had cut his profit to the bone to aid England's agricultural crisis. He had also already filled 5,000 of the 13,000 back orders for his tractors in the United States.

Within another three months, Ford had more than doubled his production rate. By July 1, he was building 131 tractors a day.

The Fordson was not a perfect tractor. But it was small, light, strong, highly maneuverable, and extremely affordable. It weighed 2,710 pounds, it could pull 2,180 pounds, and before Ford declared war on International Harvester, his Fordson sold for $785. By the end of 1918, he had sold 34,167 of his tractors.

In 1918, International Harvester marketed two tractors: the Titan 10–20 and the International 8–16. Sales of the two machines totaled 20,837, putting International Harvester in second place behind Ford for total sales.

Deere & Company had a long way to go to finish second to Ford; total sales of the Waterloo Boy were only 5,634 for 1918. Yet, although this figure was small, it was very far beyond what could have been possible in the second-year sales of Deere's own All-Wheel Drive. And the history of the small tractor, powered by gasoline or kerosene, was still young.

Frank Silloway was not disheartened. Each sale of a Waterloo Boy tractor meant a potential sale of a Deere plow. Better than that, it was common knowledge that Ford had no

"The Waterloo tractor is of a type which the average farmer can buy. We should have a satisfactory tractor at a popular price, and not a high-priced tractor built for the few. Here we have an opportunity to, overnight, step into practically first place in the tractor business."

—Frank Silloway

plans to manufacture his own implements. The 34,000-plus buyers of Fordson tractors had to use someone else's plows.

Deere's All-Wheel Drive and the Waterloo tractors were designed to use three-bottom plows. However, Harold Dineen, John Deere Plow Works' manager, reacted quickly and set his development engineers to work producing a new, lightweight, two-bottom plow. It was conceived for the smaller tractors, specifically for the Fordson. When completed, Dineen's new plow weighed 410 pounds, which was 170 pounds lighter than the Oliver plow Ford had first examined. Silloway, Theo Brown, and Dineen anxiously courted Ford. They wanted Ford to select John Deere plows as the recommended implement for the Fordson.

Again, board reluctance intervened. This time, Charles Webber expressed disdain for Ford's small tractor and for any Deere contribution to its success. "I don't know but what this whole Ford proposition is a waste of material," Webber wrote to George Peek. "I imagine a lot of small farmers will buy Ford tractors and have no right to own them; a lot of special machinery will be manufactured to go behind them, and I think the country would be just . . . a whole lot better off without the Ford tractor than with it."

Webber even invoked wartime patriotism as he explained his feelings: "It is going to chew up a lot of material, and the implements that are designed to go behind it are going to chew up a lot of material, and that material might better be used for other purposes if there is going to be a shortage of material."

Overtime, as an autonomous subsidiary of the Waterloo manufacturer, utilized its own color scheme on the Waterloo Boy tractors exported for use in England at the time. While Waterloo's contrasting color was a deep red, for England, the company painted wheels and other mechanicals a bright orange.

The Overtime used Waterloo's 6.00x7.00-inch horizontal twin-cylinder engine, rating 12 drawbar and 24 belt pulley horsepower at 750 rpm. The tractor shared the Waterloo's single speed forward and reverse transmission, providing maximum speeds of 2.5 miles per hour either direction.

The shortages of material did arrive. Characteristically, Ford offered the War Production Board to take over the responsibility for all farm tractor production and maintenance in exchange for receiving all the other manufacturers' allocations of raw material.

The question of distributing Deere plows through Ford dealers came to a vote in mid-September 1918. The board chose to protect its own dealers. If farmers wanted Deere & Company plows, they could come in and see all the other products their local Deere agent had to offer—including a better tractor!

In 1919, Deere sold 4,015 Model R and N Waterloo tractors—off about 1,600 from 1918 sales figures. The R was discontinued at the end of 1919. Tractor contributions to the balance sheet recovered through 1920, when a total of 5,045 Model N tractors were sold. Production was up to 30 a day in 1920 and was planned for 40 a day to start in 1921.

The tractor market seemed to boom. Deere, Ford, International Harvester, Moline Plow Company, and J. I. Case competed against 181 other, lesser manufacturers at the beginning of 1920. With Deere solidly among the top five, Silloway's assessment of Waterloo's value to the company seemed exceptionally

prescient. Yet, no one—not Silloway, Joe Dain, Willard Velie, or even Messrs. George Miller, Louis Witry, and Harry Leavitt—could have imagined the additional value that would accrue in early April 1920.

World War I had depleted the United States and western Europe of adult men and mature horses. Farmers in England and tens of thousands more in the United States had no choice but to adopt tractors. Ford's Fordson, Deere's Waterloo Boy, Wallis Tractor Company's Cub, Case's 10–18, International Harvester's 8–16, and Moline Plow's Universal all redefined the tractor. No longer was the "water boy" needed, along with an engineer, a fire stoker, and a plower. The one-man tractor, at first a Waterloo model name, had become a universal reality. America was tractor crazy.

For each legitimate engineer and inventor in the game, at least one con artist was involved. Some manufacturers sold stock in order to go into business; others only sold stock—that was their business. In some cases, tractors were ill-conceived, inadequately tested, inaccurately advertised, and innately unusable. Some of the craftiest schemers used some of the most legitimate names to dupe some of the least-sophisticated buyers. Henry Ford was a victim of

This 1916 Overtime is number 4,582. A total of almost 4,000 Overtime Model R and N versions were exported through 1920. Each was rated as a tractor capable of pulling three 14-inch plows through average soil conditions.

Every model of tractor offered for sale within the state [is] to be favorably passed upon by a board of three competent engineers under control of state university management.

—Nebraska Tractor Test Bill

From 1913 to1925, first Waterloo Gasoline Engine Company and then Deere & Company produced and marketed a portable engine based first on its Model R and then its Model N tractor. This restored example is from 1920, number 1056.

manufacturers in Minnesota who hired a man called Ford just to use his name. The Minneapolis company was able to produce a tractor named Ford, and Henry Ford's firm in Dearborn, Michigan, had to incorporate as Ford & Son.

Unfortunately for Wilmot Crozier, he bought the wrong Ford. Crozier was a former-educator-turned-state-legislator in Nebraska. He limped the Minneapolis Ford back to his farm, where it broke down, never to perform as advertised. Frustrated and wary, he bought a secondhand Rumely. To his pleasure, it exceeded its claims and his expectations. That caused him to wonder what else was out there, how well it worked, and what he could do about it.

Crozier was not the first to wonder, but he was the first in a position to do something. He got together with another Nebraska legislator-farmer, Charles Warner, and they contacted Professor L. W. Chase of the University of Nebraska, who was the former head of agricultural engineering and, coincidentally, the American Society of Agricultural Engineers president. Chase had been engineer-in-charge at several international tractor demonstrations. The idea of standardized tests and evaluations had occurred to him nearly from the start.

Crozier, Warner, and Chase each did his part, writing, intro-

ducing, lobbying for, and promoting passage of the Tractor Test Bill. Among several specifics, it called generally for "every model of tractor offered for sale within the state to be favorably passed upon by a board of three competent engineers under control of state university management." Introduced in early spring 1919, it was passed into law on July 15, 1919.

Tests would include endurance runs, and the determination of official horsepower ratings under continuous load as well as of fuel consumption. The results would be available to the public.

Companies with nothing to fear reacted with nearly as much enthusiasm as Nebraska's farmers felt. For both, the tests meant the frauds and failures would be exposed for all to see—and avoid buying.

The first tractor offered for test was Deere's Waterloo Boy

Type T portable engines and Model N tractor engines were the detachable-head versions of Waterloo Gasoline Engine Company's horizontal twin-cylinder engines. Bore and stroke were 6.50x7.00 inches. The overhead-valve rocker arms were operated by external pushrods driven by a crankshaft-powered cam.

Model N. Its testing began March 31, 1920, and was concluded April 9. By the end of April, seven other tractors had been submitted and their tests begun.

Before the end of April, Deere was notified that its tractor had received a passing grade. Rated in advertising at 15 horsepower on the drawbar and 25 horsepower off the pulley, it had actually performed incrementally better for the Nebraska engineers: 15.98 horsepower on the drawbar and 25.51 horsepower off the pulley. The first tractor submitted, it was the first certified.

Unfortunately, although the Waterloo Boy passed, the economy was failing. And Americans watching the war over territory in Europe were about to see a strange turn. A war was coming home to the Midwest.

Ford's goal in bringing out his tractor, he said, was to ease the "producer's" costs so that everyone could benefit. Not only food but clothing should cost less, he claimed, and the tractor, more efficient and less costly than a team of horses, could help bring down the price of both. Ford believed that someday cotton would be harvested by machine. And he already knew mechanized farming reduced the cost of animal feed. But money was tight.

So Ford cut the price of his Fordson. His automobiles were successful, and he used their profits to support the losses he felt were necessary to get the tractors onto every farm. On January 27, 1921, he lowered the charge for his basic Fordson from $785 to $620.

Within a month, International Harvester felt the effects of the war declared in Dearborn. Cutting its own price from $1,150 to $1,000, International Harvester still left Ford selling its tractors for two-thirds the price.

Deere watched, waited, and then twice, in quick succession, brought prices down, halting at $890 in July.

Ford waited six months, then dropped the bomb. Increasing the stakes in his winner-take-all war against Deere, the Depression, and International Harvester, he cut his price another $230, and

Left: Sophisticated for its time and effective, the mechanical workings of Louis Witry's horizontal two-cylinder engine were easy to see and service. Dixie high-tension magnetos fired the spark plugs. External, exposed pushrods operated intake and exhaust valves. Throttle linkages from the governor to the carburetor ran parallel to the pushrods.

Opposite page: Start it on gasoline and then switch it to kerosene. The Schebler carburetors were designed as a multi-fuel carburetor. The only power output of the Type T portable engine was the belt pulley. The engine was rated at 24 horsepower off the pulley at 750 rpm.

telegraphed each of his dealers to confirm the new retail charge: $395.

In a hard economy, Ford suffered casualties. Sales were off by 32,000 from those in 1920. Only 35,000 Fordson tractors sold in 1921.

The Fordson met the Waterloo in the branch office yards and on the account balance sheets of America. It was Armageddon.

Deere sold just 79 machines.

If ever any event had made Deere's Waterloo Boy look dated, it was seeing Ford's stylish little red—and—gray tractor on sale at just about one-third the cost of Deere's green—and—red one. The Model N was virtually unchanged from the day Deere had bought the Waterloo firm. It had been introduced in 1917, and it was more than similar to the R and even to the R's 1912 predecessor. As the tractors sat, unsold, in the storage yard in Waterloo, they suddenly looked very old.

But Deere had not been stagnating. Witry had begun work in secrecy on a successor to the Waterloo Boy tractors he and Leavitt had created a decade before. In alphabetical sequence, they produced prototype designs that they assembled and tested. When they reached the letter D, they stopped.

Deere & Company's stationary engine version of the Model D was called
the Type W. This 1925 model, with its 25-inch spoked flywheel, is number
235,549, and was rated at 27 horsepower at 800 rpm.

CHAPTER 5

"Spoker" Model D
Exit the Dain; Enter the D

Several elements coalesced nearly simultaneously to remove Joe Dain Sr.'s tractor from Deere & Company's plans. Dain's death was only a slight setback as the real impetus began with the Waterloo acquisition: Deere then had a company producing a tractor that was already in demand.

Louis Witry and Harry Leavitt's D was the other element. But it wasn't until shortly after the March 14, 1918, Waterloo Gasoline Engine Company purchase date that Frank Silloway and Theo Brown learned anything about the D.

When Silloway visited Waterloo, he found an appealing physical plant. He also found a company with a past, a present, and an immediate future. The evolution of designs from Leavitt and Witry had resulted in the Model R in 1914. Over its five-year life, it was produced in 13 styles, each given an alphabetical designation, RA through RM. The RN became simply the N.

But Waterloo's partners would not have told Deere's board members all their secrets. Not until the check cleared.

At that point, Witry probably took Brown and Silloway into a room previously closed and showed them a new alphabet series. Waterloo introduced Deere to its vision of the distant future. Brown and Silloway learned of plans to build seven prototypes. They found some already being assembled.

Internally, the new series was referred to as the Style A. Externally, it was like nothing Silloway had seen at Waterloo before. This machine was smaller than Waterloo's current production models. Its wheelbase was shorter, and its horizontal twin-cylinder engine was reversed on the frame, the crankshaft now at the rear. Its chassis was lower to the ground.

"There is a national demand for tractors. We do not have to create it. And when a suitable tractor is built at a reasonable price to the consumer, it can be sold."

—Leon Clausen

For Witry to keep accurate testing records, each prototype was given a serial number. The Style A tractors began with number 100. When the next generation was produced, incorporating the corrections and improvements indicated from work on Style A numbers 101 through 106, Deere—now the owner of the new project—continued the alphabetical designations, and Style B tractors began their numbering at 200. Another seven were built and tested. They evolved into Style C tractors, whose numbers began with 300. Two were built by April 1922, when another 10 were ordered. By that time, Deere felt that it had it pretty close to right.

From the Waterloo Boy Model N to the last Style C tractors, overall length had shrunk from 132 inches to 109 inches. Weight had dropped from 6,200 pounds to just about 4,000 pounds. Yet, improvements in carburetion, intake and exhaust valves, manifolds, and engine bearings increased drawbar horsepower from 16 to 22.5 out of what was basically the same 6.5x7.0-inch engine.

When Deere & Company's Experimental Department produced the first Style D tractor, it numbered it 400. Waterloo Gasoline Engine Company had begun its production Model R at serial number 1,026 and reserved serial numbers to 9,999. Model N production began at serial number 10,020 and was into the 20,000s by 1921. For the N, serial numbers were reserved as high as 30,000. Deere believed that demand would end before that point. The company planned to introduce its new Style D tractor beginning with the 30,000 series.

Tractor 30,400 was the only prototype of the Style D. Everyone was satisfied with what they saw, and production began with 30,401. However, sales success being something that a manufacturer never questions or interrupts, production of Waterloo

Model N tractors reached 30,400. So, Deere's registrars interrupted a block of serial numbers further on, and numbers 31,320 through 31,411—92 serial numbers—were set aside for the last of the Ns.

The evolution of the tractor from the Model N to the Model D—as the Style D of course came to be known—was not without fits and starts, trials and tribulations, questions and debates. Witry's concept was influenced by Deere's competition.

J. I. Case Plow Works had absorbed a Case family member into its board and his business into its conglomeration shortly after the turn of the century. But by 1915, H. M. Wallis had replaced his first gargantuan Bear tractor with the Cub. The Cub featured a unit frame design, which incorporated the engine, transmission, and running gear into one housing. It completely enclosed those moving parts, isolating them from weather and the destructive dust of the farm field.

The 1916 Fordson followed suit, although Ford claimed he'd used the unit frame principle first. International Harvester's International 8–16 was introduced in 1917. Moline Plow Company, which had bought the Universal Tractor Company in 1915, sold the Universal Model D beginning in 1918, outfitted with electric lights, starter, and governor. Allis-Chalmers introduced its Model 6–12 in 1919, which was a tractor quite similar to Moline's Universal. Hart-Paar was poised to introduce its compact Model 10–20 in 1921.

Deere considered the unit frame, and then adopted it. Some of the prototype tractors were nicknamed bathtub tractors because of the configuration. Other considerations arose. Deere's first production tractor, Dain's All-Wheel Drive, had used McVicker's four-

JOHN DEERE FARM TRACTOR
MODEL D 15-27

**THE SIMPLE TRACTOR THAT IS LIGHT IN WEIGHT AND SMALL IN
DIMENSIONS, BUT BIG IN POWER**

Above: A 1925 Model D 15-27. This model features a 24-inch diameter spoked flywheel. Compare to the 26-inch flywheel opposite. Solid flywheels came in 1926.

Opposite page: Kenny Layher, left, and his father, Lester, concluded the corn was still too moist to harvest even as more rain approached. Their 1923 Model D ignored the weather—just as Deere tractors have done for decades. This is one of the earliest known, number 30,410, the tenth D built. Its "ladder-side" radiator and 26-inch spoked flywheel are obvious visual clues.

cylinder engines. The Fordson, the Universal, and the 8–16 also used fours. But Deere's Waterloo tractors stayed with two-cylinder power. In mid-1922, when board member Leon Clausen recom-mended that 10 additional Style C tractors be built for further testing, he once again raised the question of two-cylinder engines versus fours. Charles Webber quickly responded.

The tractor war with Ford and International Harvester had hurt Deere badly. A poor spring crop had further eroded the few tractor and implement sales anticipated. Deere had laid off employees and cut the salaries of those who remained. It had no money to develop and test a new four-cylinder engine. And it still had a large stockpile of the Model N engines on hand. It was not technology, but finance, that dictated the decision.

In mid-1923, it came time to retire the N and give birth to the new Model D. In 1921, Deere had manufactured 786 tractors and sold only 79; in 1922, it built only 307. Plans for 1923, already shaping up to be another bad year, were being revised downward.

Yet, Clausen pressed hard for a first-year production of 1,000 of the new tractors. Wayne Broehl quoted the board minutes and Clausen's summation: "There is a national demand for tractors. We do not have to create it. And when a suitable tractor is built at a reasonable price to the consumer, it can be sold."

Pointing out that Ford's sales figures—for a suitable tractor at a reasonable price—were in the tens of thousands, Clausen won.

And then, so did Deere, as well.

In 1923 and 1924, 880 Model Ds were manufactured. The farmer's response was nearly as great as Clausen had predicted. Although the tractor division showed a loss in 1923 and again in

1924, it turned a profit in 1925, and the figures grew from there.

Two significant elements affected this reversal of fortunes. The first was mechanical: ongoing research and development. Even after introducing the new tractors, Deere & Company continued to test it and advance its development.

The first 50 tractors appeared with a welded front axle and left-side steering. The flywheel—used for starting instead of a crank, as had been employed on the Waterloo Boys—was a 26-inch diameter open affair with six spokes. It was bolted onto the drive-shaft. The engine was the improved version of the Waterloo Model N's, the 6.5x7.0-inch horizontal two-cylinder, still coupled to a

Right: Left-hand steering and a four-hole steering wheel: sure signs of the earliest 1923 Model D tractors. Deere & Company reduced the number of holes—slots—in the steering wheel each successive year: three in 1924, two in 1925, and, for no known reason, they skipped the single and in 1926 went to a solid-spoke wheel.

Opposite page: The first 50 Model D tractors also used what is referred to as the "fabricated" front axle, quite apparently pieced together from steel rods and plates. Beginning with number 30,451, the Ds used a cast front axle that was far stronger.

two-speed transmission.

Almost immediately, changes began to appear. Beginning with the 51st model produced, the front axle was a casting. At the beginning of 1925, a 24-inch diameter spoked flywheel replaced the 26-inch original. The first production of 1926 saw a new solid flywheel keyed onto the driveshaft. Enough farmers had broken arms and lost hands between the spokes that this change was necessary. In 1927, the driveshaft was splined to hold the flywheel, and the engine bore was enlarged from 6.5 inches to 6.75 inches. In 1931, the steering wheel and gear moved to the tractor's right side, and the engine governor speed was increased from 800 rpm to 900 rpm. In 1935, while many Deere competitors were going to four-speed transmissions, the Model D got a third forward gear.

The second element that benefited Deere's tractor profits was human: a nephew of John Deere's son Charles, Charles Deere Wiman. According to Broehl, Wiman had joined the firm in 1915 as a line employee in the shop, earning 15 cents per hour. In 1919, he was named to the board, and in 1924, he was appointed director of manufacturing, in time for the first wave of new tractors. Wiman was well liked and respected by both shop workers and board members. With the new tractor's increasing influence on company profit and policy, he continually promoted product improvements and new developments. In 1925, he increased tractor production to 3,900 machines.

Wiman looked carefully at the Model D's capabilities and its limitations. He concluded that it had plenty of both.

This machine evolved because farmers—and magazine editors—wanted a tractor to do first and second cultivation. International Harvester introduced its Farmall, and Deere set engineer Theo Brown to develop an all-purpose tractor. Three prototypes were completed in 1926, 24 in 1927, and 75 in 1928, known as the Model C.

CHAPTER 6

Model C Experimental
C Sounds Like D, So Call It GP

When George Schutz and John Molstad—the branch manager and territory salesman, respectively, for Deere & Webber—traveled through the Dakotas in late 1916, they talked with farmers about tractors. They learned but yet didn't recognize one issue that would affect tractor sales for another decade.

"If a customer has trouble," the salesman at Fargo Implement Company of Fargo North Dakota, told them, "and they all seem to have an undue amount, he will blame the Fargo Implement Company." But the farmers not only blamed the implement salespeople, they blamed the tractor itself. Farmers who, as Charles Webber put it, "have no right to own them" would buy tractors and, not knowing how to use them, would have troubles. And after church on Sunday, they would give witness to the weekday failures of the machine, without recognizing, or acknowledging, their own failures.

This phenomenon was never identified as a case of the poor artisan who blames the tools. Instead, it was always related as the actual experience of a competent neighbor: "This tractor didn't work"; "Don't buy anything that company makes." But until the firm establishment of the Nebraska tests, the fault often did lie with the tools. And even after the strength of the tests began weeding out the failures and frauds, tractors still caused problems. They could not be all things to all farmers.

For all the improvements in the farm tractor during the first 20 years of the twentieth century, it was still a machine for pulling. Its use was limited to starting the season pulling a two-bottom plow or a 10-plow gang and ending the season pulling a combine or a binder. The gasoline or kerosene tractor, as it had evolved from the first steam traction engines, was suitable for the land and crops between the Mississippi River and the Rocky Mountains, along with a large patch in central California.

> *"No more horsepower could be built into our present Model D tractor without a pretty thorough redesign throughout."*
>
> –Charles Deere Wiman

But farmers raising corn in the East and cotton in the South needed to cultivate their rows during the middle of the growing season. Tractors could not do that. In an article in the March 16, 1922, issue of Automotive Industries, quoted in Robert Williams' 1987 book Fordson, Farmall, and Poppin' Johnny: A History of the Farm Tractor and Its Impact on America, J. S. Clapper, president of the Toro Motor Company of Minneapolis, wrote an appeal for "The All-Purpose Tractor on the Modern Farm":

"The most difficult operation in farming is the first and second cultivation of the tender plants and, unless the operator has an entirely unobstructed view of the rows and the machine has the necessary flexibility so that cultivating teeth or shovels will respond promptly to every move of the operator, good clean cultivation is not possible without injury to the plants. Unless we can give the farmer a machine capable of doing equally as good cultivation, easier and more economical to operate and which will perform the work faster with less effort on his part than can be done with horses, we have little argument to persuade him that he should motorize his farm."

It was these considerations as well as the post–World War I depression that limited tractor sales. But some things were soon to change.

On July 17, 1923, McCormick-Deering Division of International Harvester registered the name Farmall. The term had been used internally on prototype cultivators and tractors since November 1919, and since then, 23 development tractors, all called Farmall, had been produced. Two of these eventually accumulated more than 15,000 hours of use, and the final tests confirmed International Harvester's faith in the model. Initial production for the machine's

1924 introductory year was set at 200, with each unit to be offered at $825, which reflected a substantial loss, since these were still largely handmade tractors. In the first four months, 111 sold. At year-end, the price was increased to $950 as production went from hand assembly to the regular production line.

To Charles Wiman, this new Farmall, with its narrow front wheel, wide rear tread, and high-rear-axle ground clearance—and its complete line of implements, including a front-mounted four-row cultivator for $88.50—represented bold handwriting on the wall. Although the Model D was sure to succeed, Wiman studied the Farmall and ordered Theo Brown, by then head of the John Deere Plow Works Experimental Department, to design a similar machine.

In less than a year, Brown had three running prototypes. The tractors were novel in several ways. Although they were rated only as two-plow tractors (the Model D was rated at three), Brown had adopted Joe Dain's power lift mechanism. This enabled the farmer to use engine power to lift the cultivator or planter, as Dain's machine had lifted its center-mounted plows.

Brown's other novelty became a liability. For some reason, he chose, from the start, to configure the new all-crop tractor as a three-row cultivator (the Farmall operated with two- or four-row cultivators). This prompted a lot of head scratching and concern. H. B. McKahin, planter works manager, tested it in Texas in 1926 and pronounced it "unpopular." Division Sales Manager C. H.

Hornburg tested it, again in Texas, in 1927, and was "not yet convinced that the three-row idea [was] right."

In 1926, production of International Harvester's Farmall had exceeded 4,000, and in 1927, it would top 9,000 tractors. McCormick-Deering and International Harvester dealers had tractors for sale, and Deere branch agents were growing impatient. For Wiman, these were tense times. The Brown prototype tractors, known as Model Cs, were coming up short on horsepower. The three-row cultivator was clearly a question mark. Should Wiman order everything redesigned and retested? This process would take another two years and destroy Deere & Company's place in the market. Or should he go ahead with production and, as before, continue to develop and improve the product in the regular production series? Wiman decided to go ahead with Brown's design and let it evolve during its production run.

Serial numbers of the experimentals began with number 200,001. This example, number 200,109, was one of the handful of 112 development tractors that escaped factory recall, reconstruction, and renumbering as Model GPs.

One more question needed consideration. Was Deere to stick with its alphabetical heritage? The Farmall name had undeniable appeal, and it quickly explained what the tractor was meant to do. Would the farmer distinguish between Deere's Model D and Model C? Names such as Powerfarmer and Farmrite were suggested. Frank Silloway questioned how the Model C, less powerful and less capable than the D, could be called a Powerfarmer. Yet, he had heard objections from some of the branch salespeople who worried that over the telephone, C sounded like D and the two might be

Left: Experimental tractors used experimental parts. These parts were first cast without numbers. After successful trials, they earned their parts numbers. Parts modified from existing stock often had an X cast in, pending their approval. These then got a C prefix that continued when the tractor was produced as the GP.

Opposite page: The Model C used much of the Model D's running gear, with Deere's 6.75x7.00-inch two-cylinder engine introduced in 1927. However, the new three-speed transmission was tested on these tractors for production for 1929. Wico's high-tension magneto was driven off the crankshaft. The engine rated 10 drawbar and 20 belt-pulley horsepower.

misunderstood. So it was suggested that Deere call the new model the GP, for General Purpose, which would confuse no one.

Wiman agreed, and, in early 1928, after much board discussion, he authorized an additional $3.9 million for construction of more manufacturing facilities at the Waterloo works. Several board members objected to this expenditure, but Charles Webber argued that "the tractor business is so definitely connected with our other tools...[that] we have suffered very much by not having sufficient tractors this year."

By October, GP production was up to 25 per day. But the tractor's lack of power was an increasing concern. Also known as a Model 10–20, the GP was actually expected to produce 25-horsepower belt. Yet, three weeks worth of production engines had only shown 22.6 horsepower on test benches.

Deere's concern went further than the new GP. For 1928, the Model D cylinder bore was increased 0.25 inch, which raised power output to 28 horsepower on the drawbar, 36 horsepower on the belt. But International Harvester had increased the bore of its 15–30 tractor the same amount and was reportedly adding 5 horsepower and 12 horsepower to its drawbar and pulley ratings, respectively.

As Wayne Broehl reported, "Wiman even brought this issue to the Board, telling them that he had 'given some thought to the proposition of making a straight two-plow tractor to be known as the Model B to either replace the GP or be an addition to the line.'" What's more, Wiman understood the engineering. "No more horsepower could be built into our present Model D tractor without a pretty thorough redesign throughout," he stated.

For the GP, history repeated itself. Stories that Schutz and Molstad had heard a decade earlier about overworked tractors breaking down came back to haunt Deere. GPs had troubles. GPs were failing. Some had required rebuilds in the fields. And the three-row cultivator was a failure. In addition, the steering was difficult and inaccurate. Most GPs used a steering shaft that ran up the side of the engine. Road steering was a challenge.

Brown and his design team returned to the trenches, and in a one-year crash program, produced a Farmall clone, the General-Purpose Wide-Tread (GP-WT). Its front axle, narrowed, fit between two rows, and its rear axle, widened like the Farmall's, straddled the same two rows. The first 23 prototype GP tricycles were completed in mid-April 1929, and production of the Wide-Tread model had begun even before that. In time for spring planting, the GP-WT was available. In the South and in the Midwest, it met with immediate acceptance.

Deere's concern now was only with International Harvester. Henry Ford, who had declared war on all competitors, had been defeated. The faults of his little Fordson had finally overcome the price differentials, and by the end of 1928, Ford had conceded defeat and left the tractor business. Deere remained in second place, but now it was runner-up to International Harvester.

Deere & Company's General Purpose tractors appeared first in 1928 in tricycle configuration. Many had cast front wheels at the start, which were also known as "Texas wheels." These dish-shaped wheels shed sticky gumbo soil but would clot and ball up in softer soil conditions where spoked wheels with guide bands were preferred.

CHAPTER 7

Model GP and Specials
Potatoes in Maine, Apples in Washington

It was a vicious circle. As tractors became more general in purpose, all-crop in execution, the branch agents and implement dealers conceived of even more specialized requirements and uses for them.

Of the 23 original GP tricycles, about half a dozen were assembled with narrower rear wheel rims—8-inch treads instead of 10s. Square holes were tapped into the steel rims, for 16 lugs. The rear track was 68 inches, not 74 inches. These examples were customized to meet the needs of the potato growers in Maine.

Following the first six potato farm "prototypes," the factory issued an order to Manufacturing in mid-November 1929 to assemble an estimated 150 Series P tractors a year. Known as decision copy, the authorizing document was originally circulated among those who needed to know, and eventually published in the Two-Cylinder Club's *Collector Series*, volume 1. It said:

"To meet the requirements for potato culture we will make a Series 'P' tractor which is similar to the General Purpose Wide-Tread tractor except change wheel tread to 68 inches by making shorter right and left quills, differential shaft, right and left brake cams and drawbar. Use standard front wheels 24x4 inches equipped with standard General Purpose guide bands. Use 44x8-inch rear wheels punched so that either 24 or 16 lugs per wheel may be used. . . . Power shaft and lift complete will be furnished standard with tractor, a new lift pendulum being required for the Series 'P' tractor. . . .

"A new serial number plate will be used, numbers beginning with P5000."

According to Two-Cylinder Club research, production reached 203 in 1930, but that was the only year the Series P was built. During its run, a new rear wheel was designed with a 3-inch offset,

"Believe me, Deere didn't plan for any other kind of tractor adaptation when they designed their Model B. It was really just lucky!"

—Jesse Lindeman

and it could be reversed on the shaft to accomplish the 68-inch tread width. The parallel front wheels, known as the "bedding" front end, standard on the P tractors, was retained as an option after the series was discontinued. Shipping records indicated that all 203 Series P tractors produced were delivered to branch houses or directly to farmers in the American Northeast and in eastern Canada.

Another decision copy, dated January 22, 1931, marked the end of the Series P. Again, from Two-Cylinder Club research comes the exact wording: "To standardize equipment and to continue to furnish a tractor for potato cultivation we will discontinue production of the Series 'P' tractor and furnish instead a Wide-Tread tractor with special offset wheels to provide the same tread as now obtained with the Series 'P.'"

A distant 2,800 miles due west of the potato farms in Maine, one customer in Yakima, Washington, ordered his tractors without any wheels at all.

In 1920, when Jesse Lindeman was barely 20 years old, he moved from western Iowa to central Washington. Two years later, when his brother Harry turned 20, he joined Jesse, and together, they started Lindeman Power Equipment Company, selling Holt crawlers and harvesters in the valley of the Yakima and Naches rivers. In 1925, when C. L. Best Tractor Company and Holt Manufacturing Company merged assets and dealers, the Lindemans missed the cut. They quickly picked up a Cletrac franchise from John Lampert in Spokane, Washington. Crawlers were a near necessity in the sandy, hilly terrain where the prevalent crop was tree-grown fruit. The Lindeman brothers found few faults initially with the Cletracs, and their company quickly became one of Washington's largest dealers.

Early General Purpose wide-tread tractors adopted the side-mounted worm-and-sector steering of the Model D and Model C experimentals. Steering was difficult and inaccurate no matter which front wheels were fitted. In 1932, Deere introduced "overhead steering," which removed the slack and allowed a narrower hood for improved visibility.

"What struck us was that here was this wheel tractor, this Model D, and this engine burned what we called 'stove top.' And all these farmers out here not only wanted that, but they had to have crawler tracks on it. So we just looked in our warehouse and found a used set of Best 30 tracks and rollers. It was a simple enough thing to do, but it was ugly!"

—Jesse Lindeman

In 1930—after adding younger brother Ross but losing brother Harry to a fatal auto accident—Lindeman became a John Deere full-line dealer. Rollin White, Cletrac's owner, had begun "tinkering" with his company and its machines, and the quality had slipped. The Deere Model D impressed the Lindemans.

"What struck us," Jesse recalled, shortly before his death in 1992, "was that here was this wheel tractor, this Model D, and this engine burned what we called 'stove top,' this 'fuel' that cost 6.5 cents a gallon, no tax. And all these farmers out here not only wanted that, but they had to have crawler tracks on it."

"So we just looked in our warehouse and found a used set of Best 30 tracks and rollers," he explained. Then he continued with a laugh: "It was a simple enough thing to do, but it was ugly!"

Little brother Joe did the tractor testing, up near Rim Rock at the north end of the valley. The D crawler got the attention of farmers in the region, and two more were built. Handling the tractor was a challenge. Like the Cletrac, it turned only with the use of steering brakes, or track brakes. "Which meant," Jesse said, "it didn't turn very well. Track clutches had existed on some of the earlier Best and Holt crawlers, but we hadn't figured out that adaptation quite yet."

For a short while in late 1931 and early 1932, the Deere factory assembled eight or ten Model Ds as crawlers, known unofficially as the Model DC. But the DCs continued to use wheel, or track, brakes for turning, and although this worked, it was not satisfactory. The project was shelved, and the prototypes were dismantled and rebuilt.

Ben Keator, Portland branch manager, and Pat Murphy, sales manager, came to Jesse a short while later with a new proposition. Deere & Company was interested in producing an orchard-and-grove version of its new GP. Well aware of the work the Lindeman brothers had accomplished with their D-Orchard crawler, the engineering staff in Waterloo and Moline, begrudgingly, wondered if Lindeman would be interested in performing some experimentation and development work.

"You better believe those engineers back in those wheel tractor plants were mad as the devil," said Jesse. "As one fellow put it, 'Crawler tractors back here are a dirty word.' It was something you didn't speak about." It was partly professional jealousy—the Lindemans had done the work, not the Deere engineers—and partly product orientation, as the crawlers were not considered agricultural tractors in the Midwest.

A new production GP was shipped to Yakima, where Jesse examined it and subsequently refitted it with a modified front axle and reversed the rear axle gear clusters. This dropped its overall height nearly 7 inches to let it fit more easily beneath the apple trees growing in central Washington. This tractor also steered using track brakes, the same as did both the Lindeman D crawler and the Deere factory DC experiments. This system, also like the one on the Cletrac, was a handful. The differential speed made the outside track turn twice as fast as the braked inside track, so the tractor actually seemed to go faster in turns.

(continued on page 57)

For 1933, Deere & Company offered several improvements in the GP-WT, including overhead steering. The engine, the 6.00x6.00-inch variant introduced in mid-1930, still rated 10 drawbar and 20 pulley horsepower at 950 rpm to pull two 14-inch bottom plows. The three-speed transmission introduced on the Model C was carried over and provided a top speed of 4.125 miles per hour.

Left and above: This tractor started life as a GP-WT but on July 24, 1930, it was retagged: CX20, one of six experimental development tractors—only two remain—for orchard and grove use. It was sent to Hollister, California, not far from Monterey, for testing and evaluation. When it returned to Waterloo, it was renumbered again, as GP-O number 15,223, and given a 1931 manufacture tag.

Right: Records indicate that 445 of the GP-WT overhead-steering models were built, starting from number 404,811. The large shaft holes in the frame were meant to support center-mounted cultivators, a main reason for introducing the GPs in the first place. This model, number 405,135, is part of Walter and Bruce Keller's collection.

(continued from page 53)

Five additional orchard versions were built and tested, based on the Lindeman modifications. One was shipped to southern California, and the others went to the central California coast during the summer of 1931. Successful results produced the authorization to begin regular production.

"As Deere & Company began fitting three-speed transmissions to the Model D, it was easier for a while for us to get the newer GP tractors," Jesse said. Easier to get the GPs, and easier to adapt them to crawler tracks. "We didn't even have to change the drive! They had a chain drive on the D-O, and we had to change it to a smaller chain sprocket. And we put the fenders on it to get under the trees."

Other modifications by Lindeman and the factory also included an elaborately plumbed intake manifold, which relocated the air filter to near the operator's right shoulder.

(continued on page 60)

Above: One of Lindeman's 24 GP crawlers, this is number 15,704.

Opposite page: Later-model orchard tractors enclosed the rear wheels to keep branches from getting caught and being damaged. But this experimental was one of the company's first efforts.

Lindeman's first Model GP crawler required that he modify the front axle and reverse the rear wheel clusters to lower the overall height. For the sprocketed drive wheel, Lindeman made a pattern that was then molded at his Yakima, Washington, factory. Some Lindeman GP-Os had full fenders; others had partial fenders; some had none. Lindeman adapted his first tracks from a Best Model 30, then began making his own.

Left: Lester Layher checks radiator water on his 1935 GP-O Lindeman crawler. While Deere had experimented with crawler versions of the Model D, the Yakima-based Lindeman brothers produced 6 D crawlers and 24 GP crawlers as regular production. Steering the tractor was difficult; it turned only using steering brakes. Its differential made the opposite side speed up.

Below: Early GPs had a short, downturned exhaust pipe; later versions offered the tall, upright pipe and muffler shown on this 1929 Model GP, number 209.

(continued from page 57)

Once the factory development work was completed, Jesse again turned his attentions to the kind of machine his own customers needed. Twenty-four GPs were turned into GP-O (Orchard) Lindeman crawlers, some fitted with long fenders, and others with no fenders at all. The second generation of these tractors was reconfigured with steering clutches, which disengaged the drive from the inside track. When the track brake was operated as well, this made turning effective—and safe. All but one of the GP-O crawlers were fitted, or refitted, with steering clutches. These improved machines got attention as well, from the Portland branch office for Deere & Company Plow Works. Murphy and Keator both helped Jesse get parts and helped Deere engineers get a further look at Lindeman's modifications.

"For the GP," Jesse recalled, "I made a master pattern for a one-sixth section of the new drive wheel. Then, Paul Austin [one of Lindeman's engineers] cast one with the teeth and then went on and made a mold from that. And that was about it.

"When we got it finished," Jesse said, "the John Deere people came out, and they were impressed. And they looked it over carefully. What happened was they said, 'You must identify this as not a John Deere tractor. You used John Deere parts, but it's a Lindeman.'"

Jesse laughed. "I would have done the same thing. So, we called it the Lindeman John Deere—of course, we liked the John Deere name because it sold tractors." He hesitated for a moment. "Although, now I hear that they refer to our tractors as John Deere Lindemans."

Jesse enjoyed the honors bestowed, nearly 60 years after the fact. "Now, they paint the letters in the end plates yellow. I keep telling them we were too modest for that.

"The heck we were!" Jesse laughed. "We never thought of it!" Marketing was a foreign language to Jesse. And sales took care of themselves. The Lindeman brothers sold all they could make.

"Keator and Murphy came out one time and talked about another new tractor, a smaller one." Jesse looked out the window—a long way out the window, to that other time nearly half a century before.

Left: The General Purpose model was introduced in 1928 and was supplemented first by the GP tricycle prototypes and then theWide-Tread—versions more suitable to row-crop applications. The Wide-Tread models continued in production through 1933, and GP Orchard models remained in the product line up into 1935.

Opposite page: Jason Keller lifts the plowshares as he reaches the end of the row. GPs were two-plow rated, and the early models used Deere's 5.75x6.00-inch engine introduced in the Model C in 1928. The Model 4 plow was introduced in the late 1920s as a two-furrow version of the popular, larger Pony Model 5 and 6 plows.

"They asked if tracks could be fitted to a smaller tractor. Well, we were game." Murphy and Keator gave Jesse the sketches and drawings of the wheeled version so that he could begin to think about the project.

"So they got us an early chassis," Jesse continued. "It had no front or rear wheel assemblies. Just driveshafts and axle bolts. We drilled not more than 10 holes in that whole tractor to attach our tracks. It was just lucky!"

When he thought back to that new project, he had to laugh. With all the other work he had done for Deere & Company and on his own products as well, it was this one that would secure his place in agricultural history.

"Believe me," said Jesse, his eyes bright with the memory, "they didn't plan for any other kind of tractor adaptation when they designed their Model B. It was really just lucky!"

Only 26 unstyled Model A narrow Hi-Crops were built in 1937 and 1938. Model A tractors were in development even while the GP-WT was in production, and later GP-WT tractors adopted improvements from the As. Overhead steering and higher operator seating position for better visibility were among the obvious shared advances.

CHAPTER 8

Unstyled Models A and B
A Bid To Stay Alive

Half a century after the fact, the U.S. Department of Agriculture reported that between 1925 and 1928, the numbers of tractors in use on American farms increased by nearly 40 percent, from approximately 549,000 to 782,000. By 1932, the number had increased again, to 1 million. It was estimated that one farmer out of six owned a tractor. This suggested vast acceptance of the machine. It also hinted at a huge market left untapped.

Three landmark developments occurred in this same period. The first came when International Harvester introduced the Farmall, which some historians later claimed began the industrial revolution in agriculture.

The second landmark development came from Deere with the adaptation of Melvin's power lift for use on the GP. A Work Projects Administration (WPA) study suggested that this invention saved each farmer 30 minutes each day by allowing her or him to heft a lever rather than get off the tractor to raise or lower an implement by hand. The WPA suggested that the power lift might have saved a total of 1 million work hours a year!

The third development came from outside the farm tractor industry. Conflicting reports still add mystery to the question of who should really receive credit for the arrival of pneumatic rubber tires on farm tractors. But whether President Harry Merritt of Allis-Chalmers had to pilfer some aircraft tires from Harvey Firestone to try them out, or hobby farmer and tire manufacturer-promoter Firestone had to force-feed the concept to Merritt matters only a little bit.

Improvements in fuel economy, pulling power, road speed, and farmer comfort (Deere's new overhead worm-and-sector

A horse team was the only option that made economic sense for farms of less than 100 acres. For these farmers, the small two-plow tractor signaled the beginning of the end for farm draft animals.

steering system took all the slack out of the lower system) as well as safety were noticed almost from the earliest sales in 1932. But more development was to come. The economics of owning a team of five or more horses included using nearly one-fourth a farmer's land for the horses' feed. Still, keeping a horse team was the only option that made economic sense for farms of less than 100 acres. And in 1930, a farm census indicated that nearly four-fifths of the farm population worked a farm of this size. For these farmers, the small two-plow tractor signaled the beginning of the end for farm draft animals.

In 1932, International Harvester again led the way, announcing plans for its new F–12 Farmall, a reduced-scale version of the F–20. For Deere & Company, its own survival was at stake. The economy was still terrible. Tractor manufacturer bankruptcies, bank foreclosures, and farm auctions were common. Of 186 companies manufacturing, or claiming to manufacture, farm tractors in 1922, only 38 remained in 1930. Deere, in business more than 90 years by then, had weathered similar economies and knew that things turned around, eventually. However, to be able to profit when the money was available, it had to develop new products even when the time was not right.

Charles Wiman pushed Theo Brown and his staff to work on new products and new ideas starting in late 1931. The Model A was already in design and testing by spring 1933. Experimental models adopted elements from the GP-WT, including the over-the-top steering, the high seat, and the tapered hood. These were tested near Wiman's Tucson, Arizona, farm. The Model A, first known as the AA, was introduced a year later, and the Model B followed that in 1935.

(continued on page 73)

Left: Some of the earliest rubber-tired tractors on the West Coast rode on Kay Bruner wheels, cast from steel at Bruner's Los Angeles foundry. Some wheels even appeared on late-production GP tractors, but these were more common on A and B tractors. This unstyled 1935 Model B, number 3,014, rides on a full set of Kay Bruner steel wheels.

Below: The 1938 Model As stood 62.5 inches tall. Complaints about "side-draft" caused Deere engineers to redesign the PTO and hitch points, placing them in the center of a redesigned one-piece transmission housing. The redesign slightly increased rear ground clearance as well. Rear 50x6-inch and front 24x4-inch rubber tires helped as well.

Opposite page: This experimental Model A Narrow, number 411,874, boasts unusual parts from front to rear. Shipped to the San Francisco branch house as an A Regular, it had no wheel equipment included. The deep-offset rear wheels were never an option on Model As.

Left: The essence of simplicity, orchard streamlined tractors dropped the seat lower behind the wheel and encased much of the tractor in sheet metal to protect tree limbs as well as the operator's limbs. The Model AO-S was produced from 1936 through 1940, and a total of 816 were produced.

Opposite page: Model ANH, number 472,957, built in February 1938, was a later-series Model A, which enclosed the radiator fan shaft. The Model A also introduced on-board hydraulics to John Deere farmers, the pump driven from the gearbox. Crankshaft gearing drove the fan.

Despite an economy not fully recovered from the Depression, Deere & Company had turned the tide against International Harvester and steadily closed the gap between to two companies in sales figures.

Classic architecture, the side profile view of the pre–Henry Dreyfuss/Deere & Company tractors is as timeless as any tin-sided farm shed in the Midwest. This 1938 unstyled AW, number 487,553, is among the best of the best restorations.

Characterized as about "two-thirds of a Model A" but this one was surely twice as wide. This 1938 Model BWH number 57,718 appeared gangly with its extreme wide front end. Overall maximum width was 86.75 inches. Regular Model As weighed 3,783 pounds while the same B weighed 2,878 pounds as shipped from the factory.

"If it had not been for the beginnings of "logo colors"— corporate color schemes— distinguishing one make of tractor from another across a field might well have been impossible."

The Model B was introduced in 1935, a year after the A. Its smaller engine, 4.25x5.25-inch bore and stroke ran faster—1150 rpm—and this contributed to its higher-pitched "pop" from the exhaust. Still rated as a two-plow tractor, Nebraska tests produced 10.8 horsepower at the drawbar and 16.9 horsepower on the belt pulley.

(continued from page 63)

The Model A was Deere & Company's two-plow tractor. But it was much more than just a model scaled down from the D and the GP. A complaint about many tractors had been that their design created side draft, where the implement hitching point was off the centerline of the tractor, and the implement was pulled behind the tractor at an angle. For the Model A, both the hitch and the power takeoff (PTO) were moved to the centerline. This change came along with, and as a result of, a new one-piece transmission housing, replacing the larger original two-piece castings. This new piece increased ground clearance but also improved serviceability because of its top-mounted access plate and bottom-mounted drain plug.

The rear track width, differing for various crops, had initially been based on the horse. A two-horse harness placed the horses' hoofs 42 inches apart. Hence, most row-crops were cultivated in rows at that width. With the Model A tractor, the rear track width was adjustable from 56 inches to 84 inches. Despite the greater track widths possible, maneuverability was improved through the adoption of foot pedals operating right- and left-differential brakes.

Last but not least, the mechanical lift feature of the GP was improved by the introduction of onboard, self-contained hydraulics. The lift lever became a switch.

Several development prototypes were produced, the exact number being unclear, but eight being a widely accepted total count. Two of these used the three-speed transmission on production D and GP tractors; the later prototypes tested and perfected a new four-speed gearbox.

The next major development to materialize with the Model A was that Deere offered a variety of wheel configurations and track widths. It became clear to observers inside and outside the company that as tractor interest widened, the focus on specializations narrowed.

The Model A began production in April 1934 as a standard two-front-wheel tricycle. For 1935, the AN (Narrow), a single-front-tire tricycle, was introduced along with the AW (Wide), which had an adjustable wide-front axle. The AR (Regular) first appeared in 1936 with a standard front axle, as a non-row-crop configuration. In 1937, another letter, H (High-Clearance), was added, specifying 40-inch rear wheels instead of the 36-inch normal size. These were the first high-clearance models Deere & Company offered, and they were designated ANH (for single-front-tire models, with a 16-inch tire) or AWH (for models fitted with longer front spindles). The high-clearance tractors were available not on steel, only on pneumatic rubber.

The orchard model, the AO, was introduced in 1935, and the streamlined orchard version, the AOS, appeared in 1937. The streamlined variation vented the exhaust below the engine, removed the air intake extension pipe, and fitted some modified bodywork to better protect the trees from the tractor's mechanical works.

As the diversity of A models grew, a new direction appeared. This offered further evidence of a narrowing focus on broadening horizons. Deere & Company built a specialized tractor for yards never intended to see crops. This was the industrial model, the AI. This version, introduced with the AR and AO, incorporated features of both, including the faired-in fenders and dropped exhaust pipe of the AO and a modified standard front end from the AR.

While Brown and his colleagues continued development work on the GP and put the finishing touches onto the first production Model A tractors, they had another year to go before introducing its small companion, the Model B. This tractor was generally characterized as two-thirds of a Model A, in both power and scale. As the GP continued development, its output grew closer to that of the D. The original relationship between the two was something management, and the branch agents, found valuable as a sales tool. The B fit the same framework, and the GP was discontinued soon after the B was introduced in 1935.

The same evolution of variations occurred with the B as had with Model A tractors. Soon Deere had the BN (Narrow), with a single front tire; the BW (Wide), with a wide-front configuration; the BNH (Narrow High-Clearance) and BWH (Wide High-Clearance); the BR (Regular); the BO (Orchard); and the BI (Industrial). In addition, special versions were offered in extremely limited production for beet and other vegetable crop farmers based on their 20-inch wide rows. These were the BW-40 or BN-40, also available as BWH-40 or BNH-40. Designations and variations became as numerous as the crops raised in the ground—or on the trees.

Sales of the tractors went very well despite an economy not quite fully recovered from the Depression. Deere & Company had turned the tide against International Harvester and steadily closed the gap between the two companies in sales figures. Allis-Chalmers had come on strong with its rubber-tired Model U in 1933 and 1934. Its successor, the WC—the first tractor designed specifically for use on pneumatic rubber tires—had just been introduced.

At this point, however, all the tractors from all the makers looked alike. The resemblance was confusing. If it had not been for the beginnings of "logo colors"—corporate color schemes—distinguishing one make of tractor from another across a field might well have been impossible.

Deere's engineers knew they made a good product. But they also understood that to make their tractors sell better in the marketplace against their competition, they needed something more.

Yes, the engineers had provided hydraulics, and adjustable tread widths for the front and rear wheels. They had introduced high-clearance models to serve cotton and corn growers, and extremely narrow tread models to satisfy the beet and asparagus and celery growers. They had given their tractors every technological advance they could.

What they knew the machines needed—and what they knew they couldn't give to the tractors themselves—was "style."

In mid-August 1937, Deere & Company Engineer Elmer McCormick arrived on the doorstep of industrial designer Henry Dreyfuss to ask for help in making Deere's tractors "more salable." What McCormick unleashed— "styling"—certainly made Deere's tractors more salable. And more efficient, more comfortable, and much safer.

CHAPTER 9

Styled Models A and B
Men of Substance Meet the Man of Style

Elmer McCormick wasn't the only one who was aware of the need for style in the tractor business. It had been a long time coming. It was mostly driven by the competition. However, McCormick had annoyed Charles Stone the most with the idea. Stone had been head of the John Deere Harvester Works since 1923, and in 1934, was promoted to vice president of all tractor and harvester production. Stone told McCormick he wasn't convinced of the need, nor was he wild about the idea. However, if McCormick wanted to go ahead, Stone wouldn't stop him.

So, in mid-August 1937, when McCormick arrived unannounced and without an appointment at the fifth-floor offices of Henry Dreyfuss Associates at 501 Madison Avenue at 52nd Street, New York City, Rita Hart listened to him in polite amazement. Then, she rushed into Dreyfuss' office and blurted out, "There's a man in a straw hat and shirt garters out there who says he is from Waterloo, Iowa, and—"

"Where?" Dreyfuss said. "Never heard of Waterloo, Iowa."

"He says he is from John Deere, and he wants to see you about doing some work."

"Who," replied Dreyfuss with interest, "is John Deere?"

While McCormick waited, Dreyfuss and Hart scrambled through the Standard and Poor's Register. Then, they opened the door and warmly invited McCormick in to have a seat and to tell them what they could do.

McCormick had traveled 1,100 miles by rail to get to New York. The journey had given him plenty of time to think what he would say.

"We'd like your help," McCormick began, "in making our tractors more salable," he concluded.

"They looked around the factory to find the fellow with the biggest behind, and had him sit in plaster. And that became the seat size."

—Bill Purcell

With his short speech, McCormick began a relationship that would continue for decades.

Dreyfuss, who had been born in 1904 in New York City and had graduated from the Ethical Culture School in 1922, had apprenticed for one year with Norman Bel Geddes, designing theater costumes, scenery, and sets. In 1923, on his own, he was hired by the Strand Theaters, and during the next five years, he oversaw production of 250 weekly shows. Burned out, he moved to France at the end of 1927, but he returned to New York a year later and began to solicit work as a designer. In 1929, he moved to 580 Fifth Avenue, called himself an industrial designer, and began to work to convince manufacturers of their need for his services.

During the next several years, Dreyfuss' philosophy coalesced, and he formalized it in what he referred to as a five-point formula. It was primarily based on the emphasis of an object's function, holding that the form of an object should follow from its intended use. He paid attention to the following:

1. Utility and safety of the object
2. Ease of maintenance
3. Cost of production
4. Sales appeal
5. Appearance

A treatise in his office lobby explained the practical application of Dreyfuss' philosophy. "We bear in mind," it said, "that the object being worked on is going to be ridden in, sat upon, looked at, talked to, activated, operated or in some other way used by the people individually or en masse. When the point of contact between the product and the people becomes a point of friction,

This 1938 unstyled A, left, number 464,742, contrasts sharply with the 1949 styled A, number 639,237. From steering gear to PTO, Henry Dreyfuss Associates went over every inch of Deere & Company's tractors, starting with a "clean-up" on the early Model As.

then the industrial designer has failed. On the other hand, if people are made safer, more comfortable, more eager to purchase, more efficient—or just plain happier—by contact with the product, then the designer has succeeded."

That understood, McCormick knew he had come to the right place. His speech was finished, his goal was achieved, and so he quickly left.

After a night in the Waldorf Astoria, McCormick was on the

train headed back west the next day. Dreyfuss was with him.

What Dreyfuss accomplished for Deere was what retired Senior Partner Bill Purcell said recently was "a cleanup, really; it wasn't a great change." Perhaps it was not a great change to Purcell, who participated in all the "great changes" to come. But to the farmer, the appearance and the function were so improved that a word was coined to refer to the effect. Henceforth, tractors "cleaned up" greatly by Dreyfuss or his competitors, Raymond Loewy or Walter Darwin Teague, were forever known as "styled" tractors. Those not bearing the improvements made by Dreyfuss or others were still "unstyled."

This was a curious word choice. The tractors received much more than mere styling improvements. Deere machines were

Above left: The unstyled A and B tractors, such as this 1938 Model A, had a visible vertical steering shaft, and air intake and exhaust stacks that jutted upward from each corner of the tractor's front.

Above right: Styled models featured a steering shaft shielded by a new, strong-looking front grille. The air intake and exhaust stacks were aligned, making the styled tractors indeed worthy of their new slogan, "tomorrow's tractor today."

given, even from the start, fundamental design changes, and subsequent tractors received engineering changes as part of the Dreyfuss industrial design process. But Deere & Company already had engineers and designers on the payroll, and some method had to be designated to explain to the board, the branch agents, and the farmers which set of changes was new and which was old.

Before the end of August 1937, Henry Dreyfuss Associates had prepared more than half-a-dozen design studies for new sheet metal for the Model A and B tractors. A combination of elements from the sixth and eighth possibilities became the landmark styled John Deere tractor. These new lines enclosed the steering column and radiator behind a strong-looking grille. The improvements also affected function because a narrower radiator cowling and gas tank covering improved visibility forward and down. The instrument panel was redesigned and better organized to make it more readable for the farmer while bouncing through the fields. The Dreyfuss designers cleaned up the appearance of the back of the tractor at the same time, making it easier to recognize the different functions of various fittings.

(continued on page 82)

Top left: Deere's unstyled tractors featured a contoured, metal seat, originally designed by Dreyfuss to fit anyone, at least theoretically.

Top right: Styled tractors, such as this 1949 Model A, were equipped with a much more comfortable padded seat—no more feeling every bump over a plowed field. The seat covered the battery box with its permanently mounted electric light. Deere's Powr-Trol was mounted on the rear of the transmission housing and it operated Deere's version of Ferguson's three-point-hitch with automatic level adjustment. The PTO was shielded as the belt pulley had been, to protect the operator from catching clothing in the spinning shaft.

Opposite page: Electric lighting and starting were optional in 1940. Without them, farmers waited for first light of day. Henry Dreyfuss' impact on design and technology brought Deere's tractors into the light. This BNH, number 87,784, sits on a hilltop in near Denison, Iowa.

Left: The tractor seat was a matter of great concern to Dreyfuss. He once asked Deere engineers how it was designed. The men told him about Pete. He was the man, they said, who had the biggest behind in the factory. So they sat him in plaster. Dreyfuss may have laughed but he was serious about the seat's replacement.

Opposite page: The BWH-40 was intended for vegetable growers. The "W" in the middle of the seat post decal meant "wide." Yet "wide" really designated a wide front, which even this standard front end represented—two wheels, not one.

"When the point of contact between the product and the people becomes a point of friction, then the industrial designer has failed. On the other hand, if people are made safer, more comfortable, more eager to purchase, more efficient—or just plain happier— by contact with the product, then the designer has succeeded."

—Henry Dreyfuss

Top: No optical illusion, the base of the styled grille on this 1939 styled Model B Special Hi-Crop stands 6 feet above the short grass. This special was built by a long-forgotten Montana jobber, which brought real pizzazz to Deere's Model B. It is said that as many as six of these conversions were built.

Bottom: With the exception of its extended height, everything else was standard 1939 styled Model B. According to Don Dufner of Buxton, North Dakota, this machine was built for spraying tassled corn. Clearance under the rear axle is more than 6 feet. This Special Hi-Crop bears Deere's serial number 61,338.

(continued from page 77)

The tractor seat was an object of serious concern to Dreyfuss and his designers. "The farmer was still sitting down while the wheel was well up there and very vertical," Purcell explained. "This was because the rear wheels were still very small, really, and every bump over a plowed field was so uncomfortable that the farmer really had to stand. So the steering wheel was still, very logically, set up high.

"When you stood up," he continued, "you could lean against it, put your hand right on top of it. In that way, it was very good. Much better than standing away from a sloping thing which would hit you in the stomach."

What's more, even with the tractor at rest, the seat didn't fit.

"Henry asked them once how they designed it," Purcell laughed.

Dreyfuss had developed his Human Forms, a thorough collection of measurements and dimensions for a fictional Joe and Josephine. Joe and Josephine allowed Dreyfuss to design virtually any action or apparatus to fit virtually any size person. The Deere tractor seat did not fit any Joe or Josephine.

"Elmer McCormick told Dreyfuss that they used Pete," Purcell continued, laughing still. "They looked around the factory to find the fellow with the biggest behind, and had him sit in plaster. And that became the seat size."

Styled Model A and B tractors were introduced to the public for the 1938 season. Although these were at first viewed with caution by the farmers, they were quickly taken up by the branch agents, who, at last, had something dramatically new and improved to sell. When the advertising brochures and service manuals were produced for the new-looking Model A and B tractors, Deere pronounced them "Tomorrow's tractor today."

Top: It makes one wonder about the sprayer that would hitch to that drawbar. Or it makes one yearn to drive it through some urban area where status is determined by the uniqueness of what one drives. In any event, this is truly a machine to fill the imagination. Just imagine standing to do an oil change

Bottom: Welding beads along the extended wheel towers were quality work. Everything about this conversion suggests it was done by real craftsmen who designed and executed this very high Hi-Crop adaptation. Ladder rungs climbed up the rear of the right-side tower. The driver position allowed a view of neighboring states.

When the advertising brochures and service manuals were produced for the new-looking Model A and B tractors, Deere pronounced them "Tomorrow's tractor today."

Don Dufner makes use of most of the machines in his vast collection. Besides enjoying his Special Hi-Crop's ability to absolutely stop any show, he recognizes another value: changing light bulbs in his shop. Driving it outdoors, he agreed, is not for the faint of heart—or those with fear of heights.

Lindeman-John Deere Crawler Tractor with hydraulic tool bar mounted in front position. Equipped with Lindeman 6-foot dozer blade and depth adjustment shoe. Blade shown in raised position.

The Lindeman Power Equipment Company converted wheeled Model BO tractors to crawlers. This one features a hydraulic blade.

CHAPTER 10

Model BO Lindeman
Variations on a Theme

"It was a really good-looking tractor," Jesse Lindeman said seriously. "And it just looked to us as though Deere had deliberately built a chassis to take crawler tracks. No other tractor I've ever seen was that close from the start." He recalled his first impressions of the Model B that was shipped out to him, as arranged by Ben Keator and Pat Murphy.

"We had our own steel foundry, and we cast our own idlers and track rollers and sprockets. And we made our own tracks, too," he went on, "but they weren't as nice looking as they should have been, so I drew up a plan for samples and sent them back to a foundry in Coraopolis, just up the river from Pittsburgh, Pennsylvania. And they were drop forge dies, just like Caterpillar's.

"We copied a lot of that. Why, heat treating, for example. But, you know, I also had a pretty good acquaintanceship with a guy named Williams there [at Caterpillar], head of the Manufacturing Department."

Lindeman had developed a system for the GP, and perfected it on the BO, for mounting tracks so that each time the assembler put a pin in a pair of links, the next pair was automatically lined up.

"But how to put that connecting track in? Had to be a tight fit! Couldn't use a cotter pin; that'd work itself out pretty quick." Lindeman grinned as he recalled the manufacturing mystery.

"Williams showed me a slick way Caterpillar did this. 'We have a drive pin with a handle on it,' he said. When he held it, another fellow would hit it with a heavy hammer. Had a heavy anvil behind it, set the tractor right on the anvil. Banged it right in.

The War Production Board found itself "convinced" that Deere's crawlers were "essential materiel," and Lindeman got priority treatment, especially since Waterloo shipped chassis to Lindeman without rubber tires, a commodity in short supply due to the war.

"It worked great. They had a lot of good systems. Only," Lindeman smiled broadly, "they didn't have the hydraulic deal. I talked to them about that, and all they said was, 'We don't touch hydraulics. Only people who know anything about hydraulics are John Deere.'"

Lindeman learned about hydraulics from Deere & Company—and adapted it to lift his bulldozer blade. He had previously used the belt pulley. On three tractors built for the U.S. Army, the blade was raised or lowered by reversing the pulley direction.

"These were built for Colonel [Charles] Wiman. He was going back into the army during World War II, and he knew the army used the small Caterpillar D4," Lindeman explained. "What he thought was that these little crawlers of ours could be used for construction on airfields on some of the small islands in the Pacific. It was just the right size to have it fit into an airplane at that time, and it was strong enough to drop from an airplane."

Lindeman had also developed a three-way blade for the army test crawlers. Pulling a single pin reshaped the blade into a V-plow, a diagonal blade, or a flat bulldozer, With its PTO-operated winch, its abilities seemed far greater than its size.

"But the Colonel was a very dominant fellow," Lindeman continued. "He didn't earn his rank in the battlefield—it was just more or less awarded to him like it was to a lot of wealthy businesspeople—and they [the army] didn't like him very much. They ended up going to Case and had them build a new, smaller crawler."

(continued on page 90)

Lindeman built a dozen of his BO crawlers on rubber pads intended for use in U.S. Navy shipyards to gather iron ore scrap and slag from ship holds without sparking against the steel floors or cutting them with steel tracks. This crawler, on Deere's BO chassis number 333,787, was shipped to Lindeman mid-August 1944.

After Lindeman's three experimental U.S. Army tractors were rejected, two were repainted and loaned to the U.S. Navy for evaluation purposes for the Navy's Construction Batallion, the CBs, or SeaBees. A specially produced scoop shovel gets a workout moving sand dunes. The Navy also declined the Lindeman crawlers.

(continued from page 87)

Lindeman did, however, build a dozen tractors on rubber pads during World War II. These were meant to run on pavement. But their more specialized use dropped them into the holds of ships to clean out iron ore scrap and slag. The rubber pads did not cut up the steel floors of the ship's hold, as the standard steel track pads would have.

This adaptation, and Wiman's pressure on the army to test Lindeman's BO, kept Deere & Company supplied with steel during the war. The War Production Board found itself "convinced" that Deere's crawlers were "essential materiel," and Lindeman got priority treatment, especially since Waterloo shipped chassis to Lindeman without rubber tires, a commodity in short supply due to the war.

In 1946, Deere & Company advised Lindeman and his brothers that the Model B was to be discontinued in another year. Would they be interested in working on the development of a crawler for the new Model M? When Lindeman said yes, Deere made the family an offer they could not refuse. On January 1, 1947, Jesse, Joe, and Ross sold their company to Deere for $1.245 million.

Production of the BO crawlers ended at just 1,600 in 1947 when Deere & Company introduced the Model M. The crawler version, MC, went into production two years later, introduced for the 1949 season.

To further consolidate its far-flung subsidiaries, Deere moved all its Yakima operations to Dubuque, Iowa, in 1954. The 422

(continued on page 93)

"It was a really good-looking tractor. And it just looked to us as though Deere had deliberately built a chassis to take crawler tracks. No other tractor I've ever seen was that close from the start."

—Jesse Lindeman

The top of the page shows a newspaper front page:

Yakima Weather
Temperature range Thursday, maximum, 55, at 2:15 p.m.; minimum, 36, at 2:01 a.m.

YAKIMA MORNING HERALD

State Forecast
Intermittent rain today and Saturday with snow in mountains; little change in temperature.

VOL. XLII, NO. 14 — Entered as Second Class Matter, Postoffice, Yakima, Washington — YAKIMA, WASH., FRIDAY, DECEMBER 13, 1946 — Member of Associated Press, United Press Association — PRICE 5 CENTS

Deere & Co. Buys Yakima Plant

Reclamation Educational Need Cited

Northwest Project Plans Discussed During Convention

Granger Seeks Assessment Hike

Changes Sought

Property Valuations Declared Too Low

President's Order Merges Agencies
Fleming Chosen To Head Office

Farm Goals Retained at 1946 Levels

Some Increases In Production Set In PMA Schedule

Views of Major Manufacturing Concern

Lindeman Firm Slated For Expansion

Payroll Increase Looms For Major Industry in Valley

Above: It was *the* news story of the day. The headline could as easily have read "Local Family Does Good!" Near the end of production of the 1,675 BO crawlers, Lindeman employed 442 people in the various departments of his family-owned firm. The Yakima Works, as they were known after the sale, produced bulldozer blades for M crawlers and Model 40 crawlers through the years following Deere's purchase. *Lindeman archives*

Left: Jesse Lindeman joked shortly before his death in September 1992 that collectors painted his name in John Deere yellow against the green of his crawler roller covers. When he was asked why his company never did that, he excused it to modesty. But then he laughed hard at the joke on himself: "We just never thought of it!"

Opposite page: Lindeman made good use of Deere's on-board hydraulics with his crawlers. He used the system not only to lift or lower the blade, but also to change its angle of attack. Lindeman began producing his BO crawlers in 1939 and used BO engines and transmissions. The crawlers with 10-inch wide steel tracks weighed 4,420 pounds. 1,675 were built on steel and rubber.

(continued from page 90)

employees of Lindeman Power Equipment company had been kept busy producing the crawlers built there. At peak production, five of the $1,360 BO Lindeman crawlers popped and clanked their way out the door every two days from the company's 10-acre Yakima factory at 1011 South Third Street.

Lindeman had built other adaptations for customers. He manufactured a wide-tread model, for row-crop adaptations. "We sold a few of the adjustable-track Lindemans," he explained. "They were built on square tubes that we used for the framework between the track and the tractor. The track was clamped on. The sprockets were on sliding shafts so we could move everything exactly out to the row-crop width.

"We just put a short shaft in for the average person. You could put in any length square shaft in there and any length sprocket shaft—within reason—and get any track width you needed."

The BO Lindeman crawlers were adjustable. Seats would go up or down, in or out. But in the end, another technology presented a flexibility the crawlers couldn't keep match.

"In the earliest days of these crawlers," Lindeman reminisced, "they were the best way to get around the hills in the orchards. But then, rubber tires came more and more into use, and they got better and better. That's what did in our small steel-tracked crawlers for orchard use."

In 1936, Deere started manufacturing Industrial tractors based on its Regulars but with modifications developed from the firm's experiences with orchard tractors. This example, number 252,334, was the first AI off the line, on April 27, 1936.

CHAPTER 11

Industrial Models A and B
A Deere of a Different Color

Another letter was waiting to be added to the alphabet soup of Deere & Company Model A and B tractors: I for "Industrial." As early as 1926, a solid-rubber-wheeled version of the Model D had been put to use in the Waterloo works foundry, with a cable-operated scoop shovel fitted to the front. Another example pulled carts and pushed railroad flatbed cars around the yards. These were designated the Model D Industrial, DI, and a few were offered for sale in 1926 as well.

But this was nothing new. In 1920, the city of Waterloo had purchased a Model N. Hooked up to a road scraper-grader, it kept the city streets groomed after winter snows and spring rains.

With the introduction of the Model A and B tractors, however, industrial applications and requirements were really attended to. The growing need for these machines grew out of the increasing availability and development of pneumatic rubber tires. On slick pavement or shop floors, the solid rubber slipped or skidded; traction—to say nothing of ride comfort—increased substantially with shallow-treaded chevron-patterned tires from Goodyear, BFGoodrich, and innovator Firestone Tire & Rubber.

As engineers worked out the various requirements for changing

As early as 1926, a solid-rubber-wheeled version of the Model D had been put to use in the Waterloo works foundry, with a cable-operated scoop shovel fitted to the front. Another example pulled carts and pushed railroad flatbed cars around the yards. These were designated the Model D Industrial.

from orchard applications to row-crop uses to industrial needs, it became clear that the differences were subtleties, more accurately distinctions than differences.

Regular front axles were used for all the different industrial versions. Drilled plates were welded onto the main chassis for attachments such as scoop shovels, blades, rotary sweepers, or push bars. These implements could simply be bolted on by the purchaser instead of welded in place.

For visibility and operator health, the orchard-style exhaust systems were fitted after the first Model DIs. Orchard air intakes appeared as well, to enhance operator visibility. The seating position was usually kept at regular tractor specifications, but AI and BI models were quickly equipped with upholstered seats and seatbacks, since the industrial user spent more time seated than standing behind the wheel. Offset seats, and even some with a swing-away hinge, were also used. Many of these improvements were the direct result of Henry Dreyfuss' ideas.

By 1937, the industrial model line was developed enough that its own catalog was produced. Specifications for DI, AI, and BI tractors were included, and illustrations showed the industrials in a variety of applications.

(continued on page 108)

Top: The offset radiator cap was standard AR and AI issue from 1935–1941. The engine was the Model A 5.50x6.50-inch version, fitted with orchard-style horizontal exhaust and flush-mount air intake. Without cab, the AI weighed 4,680 pounds. This cab, of tin, steel and glass, was made by an aftermarket jobber.

Left: The Parsons Plow Company of Newton, Iowa, fitted many such plows to John Deere Model AI and BI tractors. Meant for bulldozing or angle plowing, Parsons' plow was extremely adjustable. This BI was manufactured in early December 1936, and then shipped to Syracuse, New York, where presumably it and its plow were soon put to good use.

Ventilation was available by swinging up the windshield. Wood doors were originally fitted to the rear to keep out the weather if desired. Since Industrial tractor operators spent more time seated than standing, an upholstered, padded seat was standard, which, as an option, could swing to either side for working in reverse.

Left: Compact quarters but standard BI issue. This Model B Industrial used hand brakes or foot pedals to operate rear brake drums located in the wheels. Standard on-board hydraulics operated attachments via the long arm at far right. The rock shaft—to regulate cultivators on Regular models—is cut off on Industrials.

Opposite page top: John Deere's own Industrial now an unpolished gem. This 1938 AI number 257,175 was the first AI delivered in 1939. Shipped direct to Cedar Rapids Steel and fitted with the LaPlant-Choat crane, this tractor did yard and foundry work on Deere's castings at Cedar Rapids' foundry. A second PTO, mounted off the pulley gears, operated the crane winch located up on the cowl.

Opposite page bottom: Curiously—or experimentally—the front axle is set back 5.25 inches from the standard location on a Model B Regular (BR). This 1937 Model BI is number 326,766. Between 1936 and 1941, 181 BIs were built.

Deere & Company's experimental development funds were tied up completing the Model A and B, so resources for a one-plow tractor were limited. The assignment was given to Moline Tractor Division Chief Engineer Ira Maxon. Prototypes were known first as the Model Y, then the 62. In regular production, it was called the Model L.

CHAPTER 12

Models L and LA
L Does Not Mean "Little"

The Model L was referred to in the earliest prototype designations as the Model Y. The Alphabet According to John Deere nearly always sparked curiosity about developments that took place between the letters and did not finally reach production. One cannot help but wonder what they were, what they were meant to do, and why they were not produced.

This production model was conceived by Deere management as the tractor for the smallest farms, which still constituted a great proportion of the whole farm population. These were the ones that made use of a two-horse or two-mule team for plowing and harvesting. The Y was designed and developed as a one-plow tractor. Recognizing that this machine would necessarily be smaller than any other in Deere's line, the board chose to veer slightly away from previous procedure. Instead of assigning the new project to Theo Brown and his colleagues in the Experimental Department, this request stayed in Moline.

One of the plants of the former Velie Motors Corporation had been used by Deere & Company as the wagon works in Moline. Willard Velie had died in late October 1928, and his son Willard Velie Jr. died the following March. When the Velie family estate was finally settled, Deere bought all the Velie plants outright. Shortly afterward, the name of the factory was changed to the Wagon Works and soon after that, the Moline Tractor Division was established at that location. But nearly four years before all that, in 1936, the plant's chief engineer and manager, Ira Maxon, was given the challenge of the new Model Y project.

The essence of the challenge was that most of the company's tractor research and development funds were still tied up in developing successors to the Model A and Model B in order to bring

"Our goal was to build a very economical product that was simple to operate and service. We were trying to convert farmers from animal power to tractor power."

– Willard Nordenson

them to production on time. Maxon contacted an old friend, Willard Nordenson, a former engineer with the company who had gone off freelancing during the early 1930s. Nordy, as he was known to Maxon and others, was primarily a specialist in engines, though, as he explained in an interview with Gary Olsen, editor of *Tracks* magazine, he became involved in the "whole product."

"An engineer didn't specialize back then as they have to do today," Nordenson explained. "Of course, the project is more complex today than it was back in the thirties. Today we have all the electronics. Yesterday's machines were a lot simpler involving basic mechanical principles.

"It was very easy to get the product from drawing board to actual build. We worked directly with customers and dealers. There were no big meetings-just small groups of us working on the product, doing our own research and testing."

As "engine man," Nordenson was confronted with the real challenge. Maxon had been given no actual budget to develop this new machine.

Understanding that the new machine would require less power than the current two-, three-, and four-plow tractors, Nordenson went outside the company to find an engine. Design and development within Deere was just too expensive in both time and money.

The first few prototype Model Y tractors used an 8-horsepower two-cylinder Novo gasoline-only engine, the Model C-66. This small twin was mounted upright and longitudinally—that is, positioned with its crankshaft running parallel to the direction of travel—unlike the powerplants of the larger Deere tractors, which were mounted in transverse arrangements. This was done, it was said, to allow better visibility on one-row agricultural work.

(continued on page 108)

Left: Following its introduction, the Model L was turned over completely to Henry Dreyfuss. By 1939, one year into its life, styled Ls appeared, replacing the early unstyled Model L.

Below: The offset steering position was an engineering necessity, although it was claimed to enhance forward visibility. Ford Model A transmissions were used, with their familiar three-speed shift pattern. Even a foot clutch was fitted, to make the small tractor seem more familiar to its potential non-agricultural users.

Opposite page: The Model L—even with its upright, longitudinally mounted two-cylinder engine—was 30 inches shorter than an unstyled Model B. The production unstyled Model L tractors used a Hercules 3.00x4.00-inch engine. This 1938 model is number 621,098.

Above: As early as November 1937, only three months after joining Deere, Henry Dreyfuss began working on the new one-plow tractor. Dozens of drawings went back and forth between Ira Maxon and Dreyfuss as each detail, from the grille shape to the type face for the John Deere name, received scrutiny.

Right: While it's certainly not a toy, this LA, number 1001—the first one built— is even manageable for young Linsey Keller. Her older brother, Jason, and sister, Amy, know the LA's just the right size to haul the loaded pumpkin wagon from the vegetable garden up to the house for Halloween.

Above: As reliable as Deere's electric start was, the company could never control when the battery died. Emil Wendel worked the throttle while Tony Dieter cranked over Bob Pollock's late-production styled L, number 641,970. Once running, the Model L had a top speed of 6.5 miles per hour while the LA, which ran at 1850 rpm, ran 8 miles per hour.

Opposite page: The Model L ended production in 1946. Meant to pull a single 12-inch plow, the 3.25x4.00-inch Deere-engined "baby" produced 7 horsepower on the drawbar, 10.4 horsepower off the belt pulley at 1480 rpm. Styled Ls weighed 1,515 pounds as delivered dry from Deere, with no water in the battery. Electric start was standard, although a front crank slot existed.

(continued from page 101)

A Ford Model A automobile transmission was fitted next in the drivetrain assembly, before the differential. This combination, born of economic necessity, was later turned into an advertising advantage. The tractor was promoted for use on estates, golf courses, and even cemeteries to operate lawn-cutting equipment, and the automotive three-speed transmission offered a benefit: it followed the standard H shift pattern, just like the family car. Also just like the car, it had a foot clutch, which was familiar and was always mentioned to remind people of the ease of driving the new Model L.

The engine was mounted on a stubby frame concocted from two parallel round tubes. These were joined together beneath the radiator by a flat plate. This cast-iron "banjo" housing was cast with steel rings set into openings for the tubular pipes, to provide a better weld and was so named because its appearance resembled that of the instrument.

Whereas the larger tractors had located the front steering wheels ahead of the radiator, with the chassis set nearly parallel to the ground, the Model Y's front wheels were placed under the engine's rear cylinder just ahead of the flywheel.

The chassis sloped down noticeably from front to rear—as though meant to allow for some kind of drainage—by virtue of low front spindles and small front tires versus a high rear axle and large rear tires. In addition, because the tractor's overall length was so short—91 inches compared with the 120.5 inches of the first unstyled Model B—the driver's seating position was offset slightly to the right, and the engine and steering positions were offset slightly to the left, when looking at the tractor from the rear. Both rear brakes were operated by the right foot, each with its own pedal. The left foot operated a clutch pedal.

Jack Kreeger, a collector and historian in Omaha, has made a thorough study of the models Y, 62, L, and LA. His research suggested that something like 26 Model Y prototypes were assembled, but only a few used the Novo. Its single-quart oil capacity was insufficient to keep the bottom end lubricated. Crankshaft and main bearing failures quickly doomed the Novo. Early into the development of the tractor, the engineers made the change to a Hercules two-cylinder 3x4-inch engine. That powerplant, basically produced to a John Deere design, remained in use through the Model 62, the second-generation development tractor, and through the 1938 production of the unstyled Ls.

Another short-lived experiment was designated the LW (Wide), which was essentially a row-crop version. This was a single-front-wheel tricycle configured with an adjustable rear track.

As each new element came under scrutiny, an assortment of paper flew to and from the East and the Midwest: the seat shape, the gear change lever configuration, and the shape of the perforations in the hood and grille sheet metal each merited suggestions and alternatives, which were drawn and redrawn.

Kreeger's research indicated that only one was built. Although extensively tested, it was eventually dismissed as a product for which too limited a market existed in order to make it practical and profitable to produce.

Whereas Henry Dreyfuss had performed only a cleanup on Deere & Company's model A and B tractors, the Model L was his virtually from the start. Unlike the larger tractors, which continued to be produced and to sell in unstyled versions alongside styled machines, this smaller utility was available only in styled versions once the later model was introduced in August 1938, one year into its life, for the 1939 model year.

As early as November 1937, Dreyfuss was involved with the Model L project. Correspondence and drawings—sequentially numbered from the start as each topic arose—went back and forth between Maxon in Moline and Dreyfuss in New York. As each new element came under scrutiny, an assortment of paper flew to and from the East and the Midwest: the seat shape, the gear change lever configuration, and the shape of the perforations in the hood and grille sheet metal each merited suggestions and alternatives, which were drawn and redrawn. Just after New Year 1938, Dreyfuss flew to Moline and met with Maxon, Nordenson, and others to discuss details on the new Model 67 tractor, Deere's internal designation for the styled Model L.

Their conversations dealt with such minutiae as matching the finish of the steering wheel nut to the finish on the fuel tank cap, and making rear fender edges similar to those on the Model 62. The foot pedals received attention but were marked for future examination: "For the present," Barnhart's minutes reported, "the design is to stay as is, but in the future they will be made of forged steel and some design work must be done on this by the office of Henry Dreyfuss."

Front and rear nameplates received attention as well. Following up the meeting, a letter from Dreyfuss' office referred to Model 67 nameplate samples numbers 37 and 38: "You will note that in [drawing] #37 we have adhered to your standard form of lettering, whereas in [drawing] #38 we have taken considerably more liberty." Number 38 was selected for use on the LA.

Beginning in 1941, the Model LA tractor's engine was a Deere-manufactured version of the Hercules that had been used in the prototypes. It was designed to accommodate a generator and a self-starter. Electric lights and self-starting were a common option package.

Immediately before the LA was introduced, production of the L and the early styled LI (Industrial) ceased. A later-version LI, equipped with the Deere engine and the LA's larger rear wheels, replaced the

Beginning in 1941, the ultimate Dreyfuss versions appeared as the Model LA, with Deere's own two-cylinder engine.

earlier version. The same was done with other specialized versions, the LUS (Utility Standard) and others.

"Our goal," Nordenson recalled, "was to build a very economical product that was simple to operate and service. We were trying to convert farmers from animal power to tractor power."

Sales brochures addressed that conversion. Below an appealing photo of the L at work, one brochure read: "A Good Question—What are farmers doing with their work animals when they purchase a Model 'L' Tractor?

"Answer—They are trading them for cattle, hogs, or other income-producing live stock."

"We came up with a machine," Nordenson said, "the Model L, that could be delivered from Moline for $465. The Model LA, which had 50 percent more power, could be delivered for $545.

"The thinking in those days," he concluded, "was to make an affordable product for the largest number of people." The Model L and Model LA summed up Deere & Company's answers to the question of small-farm power.

During Western Iowa's corn harvest season, even the polished antiques go
to work. This 1949 styled Model B, number 242,292, waits its turn while
the harvester works the top of the hill at a Crawford County farm. In the
background, a 4020 tows a loaded wagon to the auger.

CHAPTER 13

Models G, H, A, B, and Styled D
General-Purpose Improvements

At last, the Depression was over. At last, the economic upturn had trickled down to the farm. At last, the debts and doubts of nearly a decade had been satisfied enough for confidence to return.

It was 1937. As the population slowly grew in number, even while agriculture was making a healthy return in Europe, the need for crops and goods raised on the farms of America had increased.

It was an era of optimism and growth. City folks bought new homes and new cars, corporations expanded their workforces and their sales and inventories, and the farmers felt some sense of the expansion of the economy as well. Land that had belonged to neighbors who were less fortunate during the early 1930s was now theirs. It had been acquired or leased from the banks that had taken it back. Older farmers told numerous stories in the 1990s of parents who had leased their farm in the 1920s. When the hard times hit, they lost the farm, and their possessions as well. Ten years later, the same banks that had foreclosed on loans for $200-per-acre land resold that land at $200 per acre to farmers who would then pay it off in five years. Many of those farmers then went after more land again.

Deere & Company's Model D was still in production, as were the A and the B. However, enough had happened from a technological standpoint that the company recognized a need to cater to the privileged farmer who was also thinking about replacing the old Chevrolet with a new Pontiac. The Pontiac not only offered more features, it provided more power.

An automotive equivalent was occurring in farm tractor manufacture. For as many options as were available for General Motors'

Deere & Company's Model D was still in production, as were the A and the B. However, enough had happened from a technological standpoint that the company recognized a need to cater to the privileged farmer who was also thinking about replacing the old Chevrolet with a new Pontiac.

Pontiac, Chrysler's DeSoto, and Ford's soon-to-be-introduced Mercury, there was an equal variety of farmers. Massey-Harris offered a four-wheel-drive row-crop tractor, the GP, and followed it with a more normally configured Challenger. Oliver introduced the stylish Model 70, and the Graham-Paige automobile company introduced its even-more-stylish Graham-Bradley, a tractor to be sold exclusively through Sears, Roebuck & Company catalog and retail outlets.

The economy that brought growth to industry and began an upturn in agriculture also brought growing disaffection and dissatisfaction to farmers' children and hired hands. Better wages were paid to laborers in the cities for jobs requiring only 50 to 60 hours of work a week, whereas the farmers' work was truly never done. And commercial offices and industrial plants closed at midday Saturday and stayed closed Sunday. There was no 4 a.m. milking on a cold Sunday morning at a steel plant or in an insurance office.

Farmers found themselves with less help and more work to do. The tractor assumed an even greater responsibility, and the manufacturers listened to their branch managers when they reported what the farmers wanted: more power, more capacity, more versatility, more, more, more. The early Deere GPs had been two-plow rated, and that was no longer enough.

Deere, International Harvester, and the rest of the tractor manufacturers responded by making each successive change an improvement in features and an increase in strength. In May 1937, Deere & Company began production of its new Model G as a three-plow tractor. Its family resemblance to its

predecessors was obvious. The need for such power was recognized at the beginning of 1937, when the board authorized development work to begin. After a brief discussion initiated by cautious board members, the two-cylinder horizontal engine design was retained for use in the new big tractor. The G entered the market with the same four-speed transmission recently introduced on late A and B models. The new G was offered on either steel wheels or pneumatic rubber. With its three-plow strength, it was advertised as the tractor to replace two five- or six-horse teams.

But it was not perfect. Early Model G tractors, unstyled at introduction, were designed with a small engine cowl and an exposed steering column that sloped to an outside vertical steering post. This enhanced the visibility forward and downward. An engineering consideration was also involved: Petroleum distillates and some other low-grade fuels burned cooler than kerosene or gasoline. The G had a relatively small 11-gallon cooling system capacity, which was what was specified to keep the engine within the proper temperature range for its maximum operating efficiency. However, the size of the radiator that was fitted within these constraints was not up to the challenges of hard work in warmer climates.

Many of the first year's production Model Gs—something like 2,750 out of the 4,500—suffered chronic cooling problems. Later versions replaced the small radiator with a larger one, indented on the top to accommodate the steering wheel shaft. The extra rows in

(continued on page 119)

Left: Tall, slender tires were fitted to row-crop Model Bs. These 5.50x16s straddled the Roll-O-Matic front axle. This front end was ideal for the independent corn-picker, trailed behind and offset. The farmer merely put one wheel up on the mound of corn just harvested and the tractor almost steered itself.

Opposite page: The final-series Model B was introduced in 1947. It used Deere's 4.69x5.50-inch two-cylinder engine, which, running at 1250 rpm, produced 19 horsepower on the drawbar and 24.5 horsepower on the belt pulley. Electric start was standard and the tractor frames were lighter and stronger pressed steel. Styled Model Bs were produced until early June 1952.

Top: A six-speed transmission provided a top speed of 10 miles per hour yet also allowed the high-torque two-cylinder engines to pull a maximum of 3,353 pounds in low gear in University of Nebraska Tests.

Bottom: The row-crop Model B rode on 10x38 rear tires. The B only weighed 4,058 pounds as shipped from Waterloo. To best utilize space, Dreyfuss seated the farmer atop the battery.

Opposite page top: This unrestored 1941 Model HWH was the third one built, number 30,217. Deere introduced the one-plow Model H in 1939 to fill holes in its line, which the Model L couldn't do. Using a Deere 3.56x5.00-inch two-cylinder, maximum rated power was 14.8 horsepower on the pulley. "California Hi-Crops" were only built in 1941.

Opposite page bottom: This Model G was "reinvented" by an owner for use as an edible bean planter. It plants—or cultivates—eight 30-inch rows at 6 miles per hour.

Left: This Model G's owner built the front end to straddle four 30-inch rows rather than two. Modified to produce 55 horsepower, he ran it near 95 percent load all day. "All day" began at 5 a.m. and, stopping every 45 minutes to reload the eight seed bins, he has planted 160 acres in a day. This G is the only tractor in which he ever wore out any gear—fourth gear.

Bottom: In order for Deere to increase prices during World War II, it needed to change models—or at least their designations. The GM satisfied the War Production Board, and Deere introduced a single-front and a wide-front axle. In 1947, Deere dropped the M and went back to rubber for tires as the war ended.

Opposite page: Henry Dreyfuss' improvements reached the Model D for the 1939 year, and these continued in production until July 1953. When Deere offered rubber, enormous Goodyear 13.5x28 rears filled the large fenders. Fronts were 7.50x18s. On-board hydraulics were standard and electric starter and lights were optional.

Above: Putting up silage, Hubert Bernes and his daughter-in-law Becky Bernes use their 1948 Model B to drive the conveyor.

Opposite page top: Henry Dreyfuss' styling of the Model D made Deere's powerhouse look even more forceful. The 5,269-pound tractors, measuring only 130 inches long, 66.5 inches wide, and 61.25 inches high, looked more massive than their specifications suggest. This superb 1948 styled D is number 178,263.

Opposite page bottom: Wico was still the high-tension magneto of choice and Marvel-Schebler carburetors fed the fuel mix. From 1931 until 1953 the Model Ds—originators of the John Deere two-cylinder legends—used the 6.75x7.0-inch version, producing 30.8 drawbar and 38.2 pulley horsepower at 900 rpm.

(continued from page 112)

the new radiator, increasing capacity by 2 gallons, solved the problem. Deere & Company issued a product recall. Dealers replaced the smaller radiators under warranty and also modified the shutters, removing the outside lever linkage and replacing it with a crank mechanism and lever hidden under the cowl.

Farmers with a critical ear heard something different with the Model G. In fact, the sound of each of the Poppin' Johnnys had varied slightly. This was obviously due to engine specifications: The big D was the full-voiced singer of the lineup. The B's pop had a higher pitch owing to its engine's higher-rated speed. The A and the G ran at the same engine speed, but their bore and stroke differed, and therefore so did the tone of their sound.

No sooner had the Model G made its premiere than the board and the engineers set to work on another project, the Model H. It was conceived basically as a single-plow machine to supplement the agricultural market not quite fully served by the Model L. The H was a true row-crop GP. The marketing people and salespeople even proposed this tractor as the perfect second tractor for large farms— those needing something suitable for large vegetable gardens, for example.

(continued on page 123)

Above: This 1951 Model A Hi-Crop, number 681,545, was first shipped to Fort Pierce, Florida, in July 1951. High-clearance tractors were manufactured for use on sugar cane and cotton plantations in the southeastern United States.

Left: Deere's later-series Model A engine was the 5.50x6.75-inch version that produced 26.7 drawbar and 33.8 pulley horsepower. A Marvel-Schebler carburetor fed fuel-gasoline or kerosene, and a Wico magneto provided ignition spark. As with the styled Model B, the A used the new pressed-steel frames for reduced weight and additional strength.

Opposite page top: Model A Hi-Crops stood 78 inches tall to the cowl and rode on 7.50x20 front and 11x38 rear rubber.

Opposite page bottom: Production began in May 1937 for the Model G three-plow tractors. Demand for such a powerhouse came almost directly from the farmers. The Model D, still in production, lacked the sophistication of on-board hydraulics. Nebraska Tests rated the Gs at 20.8 drawbar and 31.5 pulley horsepower at 975 rpm.

December 7, 1941, will live in infamy in Moline as well as at Pearl Harbor. For Deere, its styled Model G would have to be introduced with a manual starting system . . . . it would be shipped on steel wheels, and it would not introduce the new, long-anticipated six-speed transmission. Too many precious materials were represented in those improvements.

(continued from page 119)

The rear tread width was adjustable through a broad range, from 44 inches to 80 inches. The two-cylinder engine was retained, coupled to a three-speed transmission. The decision copy, dated September 30, 1938, even went so far as to describe its appearance. *Two-Cylinder* magazine reproduced the memo:

Section IV. Desirable Mechanical Features
G. Appearance
The tractor follows in appearance that of our styled model "A" and "B" tractors, with simple external lines carefully laid out to bring out the impression of ruggedness and strength.

Prototypes for the Model H were known as the OX Series, although according to the Two-Cylinder Club's research, the OX designation was also used for other, later, non–H Model experimentals. To further confuse things, OX prototypes of the Model H appeared in both styled and unstyled versions. One curious unstyled prototype sported an inclined steering shaft ahead of the radiator and a matching parallel-angled steering wheel pedestal. It looked very rakish, as though swept back by the wind or speed.

After a series of development models, the tractor began production in mid-January 1939, built only as a dual-front-wheeled tricycle.

A year later, a single-front-wheeled variation on the Model H, known as the HN (Narrow), was authorized. This version was "better adapted to the cultivation of vegetables, which are planted in rows of 28 inches or less." The first successful experiment had been built two months before. Such was the previous high level of development that only the one single HN prototype was completed. The next tractors built were the first regular production models.

In mid-April 1941, another variation was approved: the HWH (Wide High-Clearance). Again, the Two-Cylinder Club's research on the Model H reproduced the decision copy, this time from April 11, 1941: "To meet the demand from the field for high clearance adjustable tread front wheels on the Model 'H' tractor, we will adopt an 'HWH' tractor similar to the present 'AWH' and 'BWH' tractors. To obtain additional clearance under the rear axle, we will change the rear wheel with tires from 7-32 to 8-38." This changed the tractor's visual angle of attitude from nose-up with the HW (Wide) or the HN, to nose-down with the HWH or later, the HNH(Narrow High-Clearance).

The front axle width could be varied by 12 inches. The first prototype was completed—like the HN—nearly two months before announcement and production. On May 27, the decision was published to produce a narrow high-clearance version, HNH. Production for the two series continued only through mid-1942.

Model G Hi-Crops were built only from 1951 to mid-January 1953. Maurice Horn's 1953 Hi-Crop, number 63,674, was originally shipped to Louisiana just after New Year's where many Hi-Crop tractors ended up working in cotton and sugar cane fields. Electric start and headlights were standard.

At the end of 1941, Henry Dreyfuss and his designers and engineers had caught up with the Model G, and plans inside Deere & Company intended that the new version would be introduced early the next year. Unfortunately, history caught up with everybody early.

December 7, 1941, will live in infamy in Moline as well as in Hawaii and Washington. The events at sunrise in Pearl Harbor shaped corporate policies for all American manufacturers. For Deere, its styled Model G would have to be introduced with a manual starting system like that of its predecessors, it would be shipped on steel wheels, and it would not introduce the new, long-anticipated six-speed transmission. Too many precious materials were represented in those improvements. Costs would have been prohibitive even if supplies had been available.

As it was, annual incremental price increases were now subject to government scrutiny. Prices could only be raised on a new model, not for any improvements on an existing product. Changing the designation of a vastly improved-and Dreyfuss-styled-Model G to GM allowed Deere & Company to recover the costs of the improvements.

The plans for the 1942 Model G included Dreyfuss' sheet metal works, as well as rubber tires, electric lights and self-starter, and the new six-speed gearbox. Only a few examples were actually delivered fully equipped. At the same time, the GN (Narrow), which had a single front tire, and the GW (Wide), with a wide front axle, were introduced. Rear axles could be ordered providing a tread width as great as 104 inches.

After the war ended, the M designation was removed, and the G was restored to the original build specifications that had been in effect up to the morning of Pearl Harbor.

Another variation of the G was introduced in March 1950. The GH (Hi-Crop) gave the normal GW an additional 14 inches of ground clearance, and was specifically intended for sugar cane growers in the South. In fact, 73 GH models were shipped to Louisiana branches for sale and distribution, and 46 went to Florida.

The final Model G was produced on February 19, 1953. Between May 1937 and December 1941, nearly 11,200 unstyled tractors were built. From January 1942 through March 10, 1947, 9,920 GM tractors were produced, and from March 7, 1947, until February 19, 1953, another 41,530 styled Gs, in all variations, were sold, making total production of the G Series something in the neighborhood of 64,650 tractors. For the Model H, produc-

tion began October 29, 1938, and ended February 6, 1947, with a total of approximately 60,116 tractors assembled.

At the same time that it offered the G and the H, Deere & Company continued the upgrading and up-rating of its venerable Models D, A, and B as well. The styled version of the D was introduced in 1939, offering an optional electric generator, starter, and lighting.

Unstyled narrow- and wide-front-axle Model As appeared in 1935, and in 1937, a Hi-Crop version was introduced on each front end. The next year, Model As got styled, each version continuing under Dreyfuss' handsome sheet metal. At the same time, the four-speed transmission was introduced. In 1941, the six-speed transmissions replaced the four, and the engine displacement increased through the use of the 5.50x6.75-inch engine.

The Model B, introduced with a 4.25x5.25-inch engine on a short frame, was stretched 5.5 inches in 1937, and narrow- and wide-front models and high-clearance versions were introduced almost at the same time. In 1938, the tinwork was replaced with Dreyfuss' styled versions, and the engine stroke grew, from 5.25 inches to 5.5 inches. The six-speed transmission appeared in 1941, as with the other models, but in 1947, the entire tractor grew again. The overall length stretched another 6.8 inches, to 132.3 inches, and the height increased from 56 inches to 59.6 inches. The overall shipping weight was up to 4,000 pounds, from 2,880 pounds, with some of the increase coming from the addition of electric starting. Engine displacement jumped again, up to a 4.69x5.50-inch bore and stroke. The frame, formerly cast, was now made of pressed-steel forms, which offered greater rigidity and quality control.

As the final phase of development in Deere's alphabet series was launched in 1947, the company had two more projects ready. One would come in immediately, and like all the models before, provide the groundwork for the transitions ahead. The other offered a development so significant that it would change the thinking about everything that was yet to come.

As the final developments in Deere's alphabet series were launched in 1947, the company had two more projects ready. One would come immediately, providing groundwork for the transitions ahead; the other offered a development so significant, it would change the thinking about everything that was yet to come.

This restored 1952 Model MC drags an unrestored Deere Model 4A plow up
the hillside.

CHAPTER 14

Model M
L Plus LA Equals M

World War II forced diversity on Deere & Company. Among other things, the company produced 75mm shell casings. When the war ended, the U.S. government expressed interest in Deere continuing with that manufacture and other projects as well.

To Charles Wiman—now Colonel Charles Wiman—this signaled a need to increase capacity. With Waterloo's land largely spoken for, and with commitments for the remaining space available in Moline, the board looked farther outside the immediate area. Criteria included "navigable water," as access for raw materials coming in and completed products going out. Dubuque was selected, and the previously conservative chairman Wiman convinced "his" board in January 1945 to seek outside financing for an ambitious $30 million project of land acquisition and building construction.

Two years later, the Dubuque plant opened. Within six months, the factory was operational, producing Deere's new Model M tractor. Wiman had insisted, even as the war continued—and while the company's own varied production was substantially curtailed owing to shortages of raw materials—that the Experimental Department must continue developing new products to be available after the peace.

Another impetus for the pressure to open the Dubuque plant was that Henry Ford had returned to the game, this time with an unmatchable advantage. Scotsman Harry Ferguson's ingenious three-point hitch had made Ford's small tractor into an industry giant. Introduced in 1939, Ford's 9N was replaced in 1942 with the 2N. Although Ford's price was close to Deere's G and H, the 9N, as a more-or-less wide-front, low-clearance

With the Model M, the industrial designers took their ideas the furthest yet. Farmers frequently standing while the tractor moved concerned Dreyfuss. Was it a matter of stretching tired leg muscles, or was it simply for better visibility in tight maneuvers?

model—no narrow or wide, tricycle-front, or high-crop models existed—provided more than 50 percent more work per hour, and outsold Deere by the same margin.

Willard Nordenson was named engineering manager of the Dubuque Tractor Works in 1946, a year before the plant opened. At Moline, he had been involved in the birth and early formative months of the Model M, a result of his success developing the L and the LA. As did the L, the M mounted the two-cylinder engine upright, with the crankshaft running parallel to the directions of travel. It burned gasoline only, running at a rapid 1650 rpm.

Deere's objective, Nordenson told Editor Gary Olsen of *Tracks* magazine, was "to build a small, one-row tractor for the farmers with small acreage. It was a very simple machine." And, Deere & Company hoped, the M would be the perfect rival for Ford's N Series.

To compete directly, the M was introduced first as a standard, general-purpose utility tractor only. But its power rating created a market that its standard front end didn't completely fill, and at the beginning of 1949, the Model MT (Tricycle) was introduced. An adjustable wide front, a tricycle dual-wheel front, and a single-wheel front were offered. What's more, the Touch-O-Matic hydraulic lift for rear implements, only just introduced on the M, was doubled for the MT, to provide lift control for left- or right-side implements independently of each other.

The Touch-O-Matic was a hydraulic system control to raise and lower implements and set them to working depth. The pump was driven by the crankshaft, so hydraulic functions were available whether

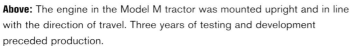

Above: The engine in the Model M tractor was mounted upright and in line with the direction of travel. Three years of testing and development preceded production.

Above right: MCs were produced from 1949 until 1952. This example, number 16,386, being among those produced early in 1952.

Opposite page: M crawlers could nearly climb up a wall.

the tractor was moving or not. This enabled precise placement of cultivators or plows at the head of a row, with the depth set before forward motion began. A large lever, nicknamed the Liquid Brain by Moline and Dubuque engineers, was mounted on the transmission case. This lever operated in a quarter-circle arc to control the hydraulics.

Seating position and comfort had been a Dreyfuss concern from the start. With the Model M, the industrial designers took their ideas the furthest yet. Farmers frequently standing while the tractor moved

concerned Dreyfuss. Was it a matter of stretching tired leg muscles, or was it simply for better visibility in tight maneuvers?

Dreyfuss inaugurated a quickly telescoping steering column with a full foot of travel. A quick twist to a collar ahead of the wheel locked it or released it. In its forward position, it left clear room to stand and lean against the wheel without being pinched. At the longest extension, it allowed comfortable bent-arm steering that most farmers preferred.

The seat also received attention. This marked the beginning of decades of care and concern for operator comfort and fatigue. The seat was adjustable forward and aft, to accommodate taller or shorter farmers. It was also inflatable; that is, a small air bag inside the seat could be filled to cushion the bouncing or to accommodate the tractor's list during plowing. The seat was tilted slightly forward, so that the farmer's legs helped hold the farmer into the seat. This left the thighs unsupported, which encouraged blood flow so the legs didn't fall asleep.

One other remarkable engineering development made its premiere on the M: the Quik-Tatch. This system, which worked

best with a new line of tools and implements specially designed for it, cut implement hookup time from hours to minutes. With a tractor in the hands of an experienced operator and with implements properly set up, the integral two-bottom plow could be attached or removed in 2 minutes. A mower, including attachment to the PTO, took only 10 minutes to hook up or remove. Deere's sales brochures claimed that the system was so foolproof it was even possible to unhook and leave the implement "in the field when coming to the house for lunch or at the end of the day."

As production was winding down on the earlier Model BO, chassis and engines were still shipped to Yakima for conversion to Lindeman crawlers. The great success of Jesse Lindeman and his brothers in converting the small orchard tractors and marketing them initially for orchard use and subsequently for construction uses awoke the board to the need to continue crawler development—and perhaps to take it in-house.

Roughly a month before the last BO chassis was shipped, an unusual prototype chassis arrived at Lindeman's Yakima factory.

Drawings had appeared in advance, and Jesse and his brothers knew what was expected. Deere & Company was considering marketing a Model M crawler, the MC. And it wanted Lindeman to develop and test the prototype.

"Well, we converted the M to the MC for them. They followed what we had done, except in the final drive," Lindeman recalled. He smiled broadly and shook his head as he remembered Deere's changes. "They did a cost-cutting deal. We had to piece in our final drive like Caterpillar and everybody else. The inner piece and then the new gear went onto the outer side.

"Well, those boys made one casting, and it was open at the bottom. And you just put the gear up into the bottom. It was a lower-cost deal—and a better lineup too. That's where experience beat genius!" He laughed hard.

"I'll tell you a little about 'genius,'" Lindeman said with a heartier laugh. "The day of the test? Colonel Wiman came out all the way from Moline to see the new MC. He was always really interested in the tractors. And he and four or five others were coming out by train.

Above: Model M crawlers were first tested by Jesse Lindeman in Yakima as early as 1946. Electric starting was standard equipment, as well as powerful Touch-O-Matic hydraulics. Here, Paul Blume crawls over the rolling hills of western Iowa.

Left: The Ms used Deere's 4.00x4.00-inch two-cylinder 101ci gasoline engine for power. The Nebraska Tractor Tests obtained 13.9 drawbar horsepower and 18.9 horsepower on the pulley at 1650 rpm. Its four-speed transmission allowed a top speed of only 4.7 miles per hour. Geared down in third at just about 3 miles per hour, the 4,293 pounds crawlers pulled, 1,833 pounds.

Opposite page: The Model M Industrial was based on regular Model M, with a top speed in fourth gear of 10 miles per hour at 1650 rpm. Production began in 1947 with number 10,001. This 1947 example is number 10,822.

"We had pulled the new tractor outside, and it would only go around in a circle. Everybody said, 'Well! How could that happen?'

"When we went from the wheel tractor," Lindeman explained, "we had a small pinion because we were driving a big-diameter rear wheel in order to get roughly the same speed out of the tractor. The procedure was, we had to cut down the pinion—in fact, we cut the ring gear and the sprocket wheel. We had to speed it up because of the smaller sprockets.

"Well, what they'd done, they put one of the regular sprockets in there and one of the new sprockets for the drive gear. One on one side, one on the other.

"So, all it would do is turn left!" He laughed again. "So, here we were. The Colonel was coming in the train station right now, and we were trying to figure out why this tractor—that was going out early in the morning to a photo session—why this tractor would only go left all around the yard!

"It was not funny until after a while when we figured it out. Then we had a big laugh about it," Lindeman continued. "But we didn't tell the Colonel about it for some time."

Above: Industrials were shipped on 9x24-inch rear tires of lower chevron depth than agricultural uses. Primarily designed by Henry Dreyfuss, the Dubuque-engineered-and-built MI Series tractors were a great advance from the D, A, and B Industrials of a decade earlier. The MI produced 18.2 belt pulley horsepower.

Opposite page: Model MI tractors weighed 2,560 pounds when they were shipped from the newly completed Dubuque factory in late 1947. Equipped with Deere's 4.00x4.00-inch upright two-cylinder engine, the Industrials came standard with electric start. Touch-O-Matic hydraulics were adaptable for roller sweeper brushes or for bulldozer blades.

The next morning, Wiman got a chance to try out for himself the new Model MC and compare it directly with the BO Lindeman.

"There's a picture," Lindeman laughed again as he told another story on his old friend. "The Colonel, in his dark fedora, is on a tractor, and he's alongside Pat Murphy of Portland on the other tractor. And he was really tickled because he outpulled the new MC crawler! He was on one of ours, a BO, and he outpulled the new MC!

"We had cut the wheel ratio in the wheel tractors easily in half. Both of them would slip in their tracks. But the BO would slip it less!

"We did that for all of them. And that was the trip the Colonel came out to buy the plant!" Lindeman laughed again.

Deere & Company bought Lindeman Power Equipment Company in December 1946, but it wasn't until 1954 that all the Lindeman Yakima operations—and many of the 422 employees—were relocated to the Dubuque Tractor Works facilities. The last day of operation in Washington, Wiman made the last of his regular visits to Yakima, to the Lindeman company, and to Jesse and his brothers Joe and Ross.

"He arrived after I'd walked through the whole factory, saying good-bye to everyone. I was told he was outside in a big car, waiting to see me," Lindeman recalled. "And there he was. I got in the car, and we sat and talked for more than an hour, just sitting there. He wanted to know about everyone, how they were, how they'd be. And how I was." Lindeman went silent for a moment.

"I used to go back to Moline to visit, and I probably saw the Colonel four visits out of every five. I'd go back there, or down to his Tucson farm, just to keep an eye on things. At the last minute, I decided not to move back there, but I ended up appointed to the Engineering Department anyway. Colonel Wiman's secretary used to call me 'Jess-ey.' One day she said, 'Well, Jess-ey, I hear Colonel Wiman is going to make you a board member!'

"But you know, he never did.

"The plant closed out here, and there was nobody working in it, just Orie Durland [Lindeman's chief engineer and good friend] and me. Going back there to Moline, they had two experimental farms, and we used to spend almost all our time there. They used to call us their 'idea men.' Geniuses indeed." Lindeman's eyes sparkled at the mention of the title.

"The Colonel never drank too much, but he loved to support a men's party. Get four or five or six of his key people, and go out.

"We go back there, and sometimes it was just an excuse for a big banquet." Lindeman laughed again. "So, everybody'd go and get half tight.

"And the ideas would flow like water."

When the "pop-pop" of John Deere's two-cylinders became a diesel
"thud-thud," it truly was the dawning of a new day for Deere and the
American farmer. The diesel was proven in the 1930s but its development
for tractor uses took more than a decade. Deere began its own work in 1947
and was finally satisfied in 1949.

CHAPTER 15

Diesel Models
The Alphabet Ends When Pop-Pop Becomes Thud-Thud

It was the biggest tractor Deere & Company had built yet. And the most powerful. And the most trouble to develop. And the one that took the longest time to get right.

But after Deere & Company introduced the diesel-engined Model R in June 1949 at a dealer show in Manitoba, Canada, it wasn't long before the company knew just how "right" it had gotten it.

Earlier, between April 19 and April 28, Model R number 1358 kicked off the University of Nebraska 1949 tractor-testing season. In 57 hours of engine operation, testers reported only one repair: a glass sediment bowl in the fuel line broke during the warm-up run and had to be replaced. The university engineers reported no other repairs or adjustments during the test. The result was a maximum fuel economy of 17.63 horsepower hours per gallon of fuel.

Deere was not the first to offer a diesel. Tests on other diesels had been performed at the Lincoln campus test site. The first had been nearly 17 years earlier, in June 1932, when Caterpillar brought its Model 65 Diesel to the university. The rated brake horsepower tests—reaching a maximum of 74.73 horsepower—ended with a new Nebraska Tractor Test economy record of 13.87 hp-hr/gal. The next year, Caterpillar's Diesel 75 beat the company's own previous record with 83.34 horsepower and 14.62 hp-hr/gal.

Diesel power was invented in Germany in the early 1890s, and perfected for tractor applications by Caterpillar in the United States in 1931. It was clearly a path for others to investigate, a direction to pursue. Deere & Company, known for the overall operating efficiency and economy of its "stove top fuel" tractors, could not afford to ignore the diesel, no matter what the difficulties might be in its development.

And difficulties did exist.

Before the end of 1935, International Harvester introduced the

"We are not making a four cylinder tractor, nor are we ever thinking of making one."

—Deere & Webber dealer letter, 1936

WD-40, the first wheeled diesel-powered tractor, and with it, threw down the gauntlet to its competitors. The Deere & Company board quickly committed resources to developing the diesel engine for its own agricultural products. Although the company competed vigorously with International Harvester, its association with Caterpillar was excellent at that time, largely as a result of Deere board member Frank Silloway's encouragement of Caterpillar's unique product.

In 1925, two California firms, C. L. Best Tractor Company and the Holt Manufacturing Company, merged assets and products under the name Caterpillar Company. Among their products was a side-hill harvester that had been manufactured by Shippee until Holt bought Shippee in 1916. The new Caterpillar Company set out to consolidate and simplify its product line, and it offered the harvester subsidiary, called Western Harvester, to Deere & Company. Deere management thought the price was too high, and declined. But the acquaintance was made.

California's soil conditions made it a natural market for Caterpillar's crawlers. But a lesser market existed within Caterpillar's market base for wheel-type tractors around the farm. As Wayne Broehl wrote in *John Deere's Company*, Silloway opened the door, appealing to the Deere & Company board for some kind of marketing agreement: "We do not desire to manufacture track-type tractors," he said, pointing out, however, that many Caterpillar dealers had a desire to sell a wheel-type tractor. "Through this Caterpillar [arrangement], we will have an opportunity to get into the industrial business in an important way."

Caterpillar supported the notion. It went further and even attempted to answer some of its skeptical dealers who were concerned that Deere's two-cylinder engines did not follow the trends of other makers. In fact, Caterpillar itself had just introduced a two-cylinder diesel.

(continued on page 138)

This 1952 Model R "Industrial-Experimental," number 10,859, (along with a twin, number 10,860) was shipped to the experimental department November 12, 1951. For two weeks, various front ends were tested and several fittings were brazed onto the frame to mount an American Tractor Equipment (ATECo) bulldozer blade. It still wears numerous MX serial number parts. Rear tires are 23.1x26s.

Deere's development of the diesel engine, a product Caterpillar had perfected, began, coincidentally, shortly after trade and marketing agreements between the two were enacted. In part, this came about as the result of Deere customers' demands for more power.

Diesels had a long history of difficult cold weather starting. The solution—reached by others before Deere—utilized a "pony" gasoline engine. Its exhaust would heat up the engine and fuel and then provide power to crank the starter. The corrugated grille was another Dreyfuss contribution. A gloved hand could fit within its folds for cleaning.

(continued from page 135)

Silloway was encouraged by this recognition, and he seized the moment more tightly. It was his ambition to lessen Deere's dependence on agricultural tractors exclusively and to increase its portion of the growing industrial tractor trade. Through shared efforts—in retailing, marketing, and possibly even research—this would come about.

Whether Caterpillar's engineers opened their research facilities to Deere's experimenters is unknown. But it is surely possible. Certainly, by this time, Jesse Lindeman had established friends in Caterpillar engineering who were willing to explain to him the details of some operations.

Deere's development of the diesel engine, a product Caterpillar had perfected, began, coincidentally, shortly after trade and marketing agreements between the two were enacted. In part, this came about as the result of Deere customers' demands for more power. The stories of diesel development brought about a return of fictional reports of multiple cylinders. The rumormongering reached a frenzy toward the end of 1936. Deere & Webber sent a letter to its dealers, Bulletin No. 11, dated December 23, 1936: "Under the date of June 27, 1930, we issued a bulletin to all of our dealers reading as follows:

"We are again receiving reports, originating no doubt from competitive tractor salesmen, stating we were coming out with a four-cylinder tractor.

"This is propaganda, pure and simple, and there is nothing to this claim. . . .

"WE ARE NOT MAKING A FOUR CYLINDER TRACTOR, NOR ARE WE EVER THINKING OF MAKING ONE."

Yet, developing additional power through the diesel was not so simple. The gelatinous nature of the fuel in cold temperatures made starting under those conditions difficult. The farmer could hand crank until spring!

One solution tried during testing in 1936 was to start the engine on gasoline and run it on that fuel until it was warm, when the farmer would switch over to diesel. By 1937, experimentation had led the engineers to try using a higher-voltage, 24-volt-electric starting system, but even that didn't pack enough wallop to heat the fuel and start the engine in the cold. Various combustion chamber shapes were experimented with to produce the required high compression, which was something like 16.0:1, compared with 4.0:1 for the kerosene engines. By mid-1940, the combination of problems had been

Left: Everything about the Model R was massive. It was Deere's most powerful tractor—and its most fuel efficient—to date. At the University of Nebraska, it rated 34.4 drawbar and 43.5 belt horsepower, at a maximum of 17.63 hp-hr/gal at 1000 rpm. The horizontal two-cylinder was 5.75x8.00-inch bore and stroke.

Below: The business end of Merrihew's 840 is the Deere Model 400 Elevating Scraper. The tractor, number 840-0984 and scraper number 502, were marketed as a pair out of Deere's Industrial department, which was established in 1958 as a separate division. The tractor sold for $6,625 while the scraper was roughly $7,450.

sufficiently sorted to produce the first of the MXs, the prototypes meant eventually to become the Model R.

Between 1941 and 1945, eight MX prototypes were thoroughly tested and evaluated at test farms in Laredo, Texas; Tucson; and Minnesota. Five more were built during 1945, and another eight were assembled in 1947. By the time the tractor was ready for production as the Model R, the starting procedure had been satisfied. An opposed two-cylinder gasoline "pony" engine was started by an electric starter. This matched a system introduced by McCormick-Deering in 1932 to start its TD-40 crawler. The pony was run to warm up the diesel engine block and fuel. Once temperatures met a certain level, the gasoline engine propelled the starter for the larger diesel main engine.

Henry Dreyfuss was involved with the diesel tractor from early on in its development. The radiator grille was a result of his recommendations and observations. With massive cooling required for the twin 5.75x8.00-inch cylinders, the fan tended to suck field debris into the radiator grille mesh. The corrugations were set at an angle that allowed them to be easily swept clear by a farmer wearing gloves.

This styling was the precursor to what would become familiar during the next decade. The only drawback was that with so much mesh screening up front, the farmer had to pay attention to what he or she drove into. The vertical crown piece introduced on the first styled As and Bs had protected a lot of farmers from front impacts. It served as a bumper as well as a design element, but it was not used on the big R.

The Model R remained in production through 1954, and something approaching 21,300 were produced. But for all its power—45.7 horsepower on the drawbar, 51 horsepower on the belt—the two-cylinder engine was showing its age and its limitations. The protests from the branch agents at the end of 1936, echoed by the factory the next spring—that Deere would always and only build two-cylinder engines—were no longer heard 20 years later.

A new series of tractors was set to replace the alphabet series. For Deere & Company, the letters sequence only went as far as R. Number designations were coming, and in the next few years, they would grow from tens to hundreds. Soon after, as they multiplied once more, they would be joined, at last, by engine cylinder multiples as well.

Henry Dreyfuss Associates senior partner Bill Purcell recalled working one day in early 1957 with several Deere engineers and a great deal of cardboard and duct tape to create the shape of the bodywork for the 840 Industrial. The result—with few modifications—remained basically the same throughout the production life.

Henry Dreyfuss was involved with the diesel tractor from early on in its development. The radiator grille was a result of his recommendations and observations. With massive cooling required for the twin 5.75x8.00-inch cylinders, the fan tended to suck field debris into the radiator grille mesh. The corrugations were set at an angle that allowed them to be easily swept clear by a farmer wearing gloves.

Above: The noise in the uninsulated cab may have prompted its last operator to mark days until his—or the tractor's—retirement.

Left: Model 840s moved the operator position to the side in order to improve their visibility and to move the hitch point ahead of the drive axle for increased traction. Sand tires, or aircraft tires, allowed the rears to spin but not bog down in soil, which deep lugs would have done—especially if the scraper carried a full load.

Opposite page: Deere's 400 scraper had a 7.5-cubic-yard capacity, which the 840 and scraper could fill in one minute. With six speeds and not carrying, the combination could reach 12.25 miles per hour.

Electric lights were standard on the Model 70s. Long work days just came with the job. Production of Model 70 Hi-Crops began late October 1953 and ran until mid-June 1956.

CHAPTER 16

Models 40, 50, 60, and 70
Deere's New Math in Multiples of Ten

The look of the Model R became the pattern Deere & Company followed for the next decade as all its tractor designations abandoned the alphabet and adopted numbers. The dramatic sheet metal changes hinted at the technological developments beneath the skin.

Beginning with the R, this revolution in design would go into the 50 (to replace the B), the 60 (replacing the A), the Model 70 (for the G), and the Model 40 (for the M), and wouldn't end until the new Model 80 replaced the R. These substitutions would be made during a three-year period encompassing a farm wagon full of improvements and advances.

Before all that took place, as the big diesel R was introduced in 1949 to replace Deere & Company's long-lived standard-bearer Model D, one question arose yet again: Should the company finally put to rest its equally long-lived two-cylinder engines? Power was the main issue. Needing it was the consideration.

As electric accessories proliferated, filling the power needs of starters and lights and better instrumentation had merely required a bigger generator and a larger battery. But hydraulics was a different matter. Called Powr-Trol on Deere tractors, it required, on any tractor, a pump that was driven by the engine. As farmers called on their tractors to do more and more work, as they were aided and abetted in this pursuit by visionary implement designers, more power was needed just to run the hydraulic pump to raise and lower the enlarged attachments.

There was an absolute limit to how far across a piston face a spark could evenly and efficiently ignite a fuel mixture. The perfection of the diesel bought Deere a little time. But the engineers and board knew it only gave the two-cylinder engines a decade at the most.

More visionary now, and willing to take some risks after

"Gentlemen, I believe you will agree that never before has any manufacturer presented new tractors with so many outstanding improvements over current models."

– Lyle Cherry

returning from the war, Colonel Charles Wiman himself advocated more cylinders. The engineers at Dubuque, always hungry for new challenges, encouraged the Colonel, reminding him they had already raised up to vertical the engine in the Model M tractor. The recumbent two-cylinder engine had essentially lain there, horizontal, longitudinal, unchallenged, since Louis Witry first built and positioned the side-by-side twin onto the Waterloo Boy chassis.

But L. A. Rowland—"Duke," as he was known to other board members—argued for patience and caution. Rowland had joined the board in 1942, six years after becoming manager of the Waterloo Tractor Works. An Englishman who knew his own mind and had no trouble expressing it, Rowland had been named a vice president in 1947—by Wiman.

Rowland argued that the time and effort required for testing and developing the diesel had been long and trying, and that perfecting a new multiple-cylinder version of the diesel—or any other fuel—engines would also take some time. Perhaps it would not take as long as the dozen years needed to perfect the R, but still, developing a new four- or six-cylinder engine could not be accomplished in one short model year.

Coincidentally, Rowland had also authored the Deere & Company official factory denial of a pending switch to four- or six-cylinder engines less than two months after Deere & Webber's branch agents sent out their own bulletin in December 1936.

The Model R introduced the concept of separate carburetors for each cylinder—or separate fuel injectors in the case of the diesel engines. This permitted greater precision in mixing the fuel closer to the intake valves and also provided somewhat increased horsepower. This was carried over into the new tractors that were to be introduced in 1952.

145

Above: The 40C added an additional track roller to the three used on the MC.

Opposite page: In 1953, the M Series tractors were replaced by the new Model-40 lineup.

Shown first were the Models 50 and 60. Both were offered as row-crop versions, but the Model 60 was also available from the first as a Hi-Crop. "Live" PTO had been adopted from competitors, and it first appeared on Deere tractors with the introduction of these two new models. With live PTO, the PTO shaft rotated independently of forward motion and was disengaged by its own independent clutch. This allowed machinery to continue its work even at the end of the row, where the tractor had to stop and maneuver through a turn.

Within the two-cylinder engine was a new combustion chamber design. Referred to as "cyclonic fuel intake," this produced a cyclone-like swirl induced by a modification to the intake valve venturi. This generated a better fuel mixture, which increased power and improved economy, whether the engine fired on gasoline, distillates, or the

newly offered—for the Model 60 in 1954, for the 50 in 1955—liquefied propane gas (LPG).

Although the better-mixed combustion tended to run cooler, the cooling system received a major overhaul behind the Henry Dreyfuss stylish grille. Until the number series began, Deere & Company had not used water pumps, but had relied on the thermosyphon system, which had served it well since the days of the Waterloo Boys. With the Models 60, 50, 70, 40, and 80, cooling was forced. The radiator was pressurized, and the coolant water was pumped. A thermostat controlled louvers on the radiator, relieving the farmer from manually cranking them open or closed to regulate air circulation through the radiator.

Another Dreyfuss innovation was an optional rear exhaust. Dreyfuss had long been bothered by the engine exhaust pipe rising up in the farmer's face, choking the farmer with fumes and blocking forward vision. In fact, at one time, he posted a note in the office offering a reward of a case of Chivas Regal Scotch and a night in the Waldorf-Astoria with a famous actress to the first designer or engineer who could get the exhaust off the hood—and keep it off.

(continued on page 151)

Above: It was a gadget-lover's version of heaven-in-the-dirt to operate a Model 40 with Deere's blade. Levers controlled engine clutch, four-speed gear shift, track clutches, track brakes, PTO clutch, blade lift, and blade tilt. Angle was still controlled off the tractor by pins on the blade arms. Electric start was standard.

Left: The Model 40 gas engine was Deere's vertical 4.00x4.00-inch bore and stroke two-cylinder, of a total 101ci. When tested at the University of Nebraska in September 1953, the crawler—which weighed 4,669 pounds during the tests—pulled 4,515 pounds during its low-gear test! It produced 15.1 drawbar and 21.3 pulley horsepower at 1850 rpm.

Opposite page bottom: This 1954 Model 60, number 6,034,848, normally worked with an 810 series three 14-inch bottom plow in the fields north of Urbana, Illinois. The Model 60 replaced the popular Model A tractors in 1952. Powr-Trol, live high-pressure hydraulics, was an option the original owner ordered, as were numerous other features.

(continued from page 147)

The rear exhaust option routed the gases through a complicated series of bends and curves, eventually blowing the exhaust out beneath and behind the rear axle. This was intended to facilitate work in and out of low doorways in barns and sheds. It provided a real benefit to farmers' lungs, despite the slightly reduced ground clearance of a somewhat collapsible pipe below the belt pulley.

In 1953, the Model 70 appeared. This was a nearly 20 percent stronger successor to the Model G. Power steering came to Deere tractors with the Model 70, and when this new machine was introduced, the hydraulic Powr-Trol system had one-third more capacity and power than was available on the Gs. As with the 60 and 50, the electrical system got a 100 percent boost—from 6 volts to 12 volts. The Model 70 Diesel again claimed the Nebraska Tests' economy record in 1954, at 50.4 horsepower with 17.74 hp-hr/gal. The gas pony starting engine was a 19ci displacement V-4.

The next 1953 numbered addition to the lineup was the Model 40, which replaced the Model M. The

Above: This Model 60 was equipped with the "Buddy Seat," front and rear weights, the Type 801 three-point hitch, rear mounted exhaust, and fenders. But because power steering was not fitted, the owner made his own by using the larger-diameter Model 70 steering wheel!

Left: Model 60s were produced from March 1952 to mid-July 1956. The engine was the 5.50x6.75-inch version that produced 28 drawbar and 35.3 pulley horsepower at 975 rpm. The six-speed transmission provided transport speed of 11 miles per hour or allowed the 5,911-pound tractor to pull 4,319 pounds in first gear at 1.2 miles per hour. Model 60s would burn gas, LPG, or "all fuel."

The all-fuel Model 70 was powered by the 6.125x7.00-inch engine that produced 31.1 drawbar horsepower at 975 rpm. The pulley produced 38.4 horsepower. A new combustion-chamber design was introduced, the "cyclonic fuel intake," which swirled the fuel mixture cyclone-like for better combustion and economy.

replacement was complete across the Model 40 Series. It included a standard, a Hi-Crop, a tricycle, a wide (a two-row utility), a utility, and a crawler, and added a special, using the designation V for cotton and sugar cane applications.

The Model 40C was a long step from the MC. With four track rollers standard (instead of three) and a fifth optional, the ride comfort, durability, traction, and tractor stability improved measurably. The 40C continued the legacy established by Jesse Lindeman. However, because Lindeman's Deere operations had been "consolidated" during production of the MC, every 40C was assembled in the Dubuque Tractor Works.

The last replacement was the 80, which replaced the R in 1955. The Model 80 took a good, big, strong tractor and made it better, bigger, and stronger. Power increased one-third. The transmission added a gear, going from five to six. Power steering was offered, which then decreased the arm size required from the farmer-operator.

The tractor range, from 40 to 80, provided power over a broad spectrum that peaked at 61.8 horsepower on drawbar and 67.6 horsepower on belt for the 7,850-pound diesel 80. The LPG Model 70 produced 46.1 horsepower on drawbar and 52 horsepower on belt and weighed 6,335 pounds. Next down the line was the Model 60 LPG, which produced 38.1 horsepower on drawbar and 42.2 horsepower on belt and weighed 5,300 pounds. Then came the LPG Model 50, peaking at 29.2 horsepower on drawbar and 32.3 horsepower on belt and weighing 4,435 pounds. At the bottom end, the "little" 40C weighed in at 4,669 pounds in Lincoln, Nebraska, in early September 1953, and it pulled nearly its own weight: 4,515 pounds in low gear. The little engine that could, did. It rated 20.1 horsepower on the drawbar and 24.9 horsepower on the belt.

These numbers were good only until 1955 or 1956. Then, not only did the specifications go up again, but so did each model number.

Lyle Cherry, Deere & Company's general sales manager, introduced the Models 60 and 50 on June 11, 1952. His detailed and lengthy comments were quoted in the *Two-Cylinder Collector Series,* volume 1. During his presentation to the branch salespeople and managers, he pointed out the numerous features of the two new models. His conclusion sounded like a summary to the assembly: "Gentlemen, I believe you will agree with my opening comment that never before has any manufacturer presented new tractors with so many outstanding improvements over current models."

One can almost imagine Cherry adding—to himself—one more thought: "And, fellahs, you ain't seen nothin' yet!"

Left: Water pumps were added to Deere tractors when the availability of copper for radiator cores became limited during the Korean War. Steel cores didn't cool so effectively and water had to be forced through to get the same effect. The pump was driven off the fanshaft, and the "fan belt" also drove the new 12-volt generator.

Opposite page: This 1954 Model 70 Hi-Crop, number 7,009,419, was the third all-fuel Hi-Crop built, assembled on February 10, 1954, and shipped immediately to Immokalee, Florida.

Opposite page bottom: Model 70s replaced the Model G and were offered for gasoline, all-fuel, or liquid propane gas power. Diesel power was added in 1955.

Another Dreyfuss innovation was an optional rear exhaust. Dreyfuss had long been bothered by the engine exhaust pipe rising up, choking the farmer with fumes. In fact, at one time, he posted a note in the office offering a reward of a case of Chivas Regal Scotch and a night in the Waldorf-Astoria with a famous actress to the first designer or engineer who could get the exhaust off the hood— and keep it off.

This page: Photo calls bring the neighbors out for help to bathe the Hi-Crop.

Opposite page: Two tractor-mounted Model 22 cotton pickers. Left, a diesel Model 70, number 7,038,481, and right, a diesel Model 60, number 6,045,466.

Right: It was a loud testimony to Deere engineering that even adding the rigging mechanism necessary to lift, carry, and dump an additional 1,200 pounds of cotton did not fracture tractors frames.

Left: If ever a harvesting device looked less like the work of Deere and Dreyfuss, it was this Model 22 cotton picker mounted atop a tractor. Yet careful study of the linkages—each integrated to both upper and lower operator positions—proved this could be only Deere and Dreyfuss and not a Rube Goldberg. The standard—or in this case narrow-front—Model 70 weighed 7,135 pounds, ready to run.

Opposite page top: Model 60 and 70 tractors had reverse top speeds of 3 and 3.5 miles per hour respectively, fast enough to harvest cotton. Called the Air-Trol pickers, these single-row harvesters would contain 1,200 pounds of harvested cotton. The engine exhaust-pipe was laid flat and shielded to protect the cotton from soot or sparks.

Opposite page bottom: Deere's Model 22 single-row cotton pickers elevated the driver far above even a Hi-Crop's lofty perch. Tractor-mounted cotton pickers had begun with a Model 1 in the early 1950s, but prototypes existed as early as 1929, fitted to GP-WTs. All the operating functions were duplicated on the top position.

A 1956 Model 420, number 93,102, waits outside the barn in Hardwick,
Massachusetts.

CHAPTER 17

The 20 Series and 30 Series
A Generation Matures

As important as power steering was to the farmer, as desirable as rear exhaust was, even as significant as fuel economy records established during the Nebraska Tractor Tests could be, the primary function and most important feature of agricultural tractors was—and is—to pull tools over or through the ground. In this regard, Deere & Company, and all its competitors, had been thrown for a loop by Harry Ferguson's three-point hitch.

It was not the success of his hitch that caused troubles, although that clearly affected sales of the Ford over other tractors. No, it was the hitch's engineering efficiency, and Ferguson's patent for using it on Henry Ford's second series of tractors, the Ns, that created problems. That the three-point hitch took a small, standard-front lightweight tractor and made it perform like a larger, heavier tractor through the understanding and use of the laws of physics—that was its success. That it was stunningly simple—once it was demonstrated—was a source of great frustration to all Ford's competition. Because that meant that anything approximate to it, similar in appearance or function, was liable for a lawsuit claiming patent infringement.

So everyone else's version of Ferguson's three-point hitch had to be more complicated.

Deere's was no exception. That is, until the 15-year original life of Ferguson's patent ran out. Then, a federal court judge refused to renew it. He claimed that the three-point hitch was too important to agriculture to remain under patent protection.

When Ferguson's invention entered the public domain in 1953, each company redesigned its own hitch to take advantage of Ferguson's ingenious three-point connection and his automatic draft control. And again, Deere was no exception.

The primary function and most important feature of agricultural tractors was—and is—to pull tools over the ground, or through it. Deere & Company, and all its competitors, had been thrown for a loop by Harry Ferguson's three-point hitch.

Custom Powr-Trol was Deere & Company's answer. The previous Powr-Trol system had been introduced on the Model R; it did not automatically accommodate the range of tractor movements over the ground. The farmer had to have quick reactions to lift or drop the plow when the nose of the tractor dropped or rose. When Load-and-Depth Control was incorporated into the description of the current John Deere tractors, enough other major and minor changes were made that new models were designated. They began the 20 Series.

Of course, many other improvements were made. The Quik-Tatch system was now capable of rapidly coupling ever-larger implements to Deere's Load-and-Depth Custom Powr-Trol. The driver's seat, which was already equipped with a low backrest for lumbar support, received a slightly raised seatback and added armrests. And the formerly black-only seat cushions were now offered in Deere yellow. As a logo color element, the seats made sense. For the farmer climbing into the driver's seat on a sunny afternoon in August, it made even better sense to have something more reflective than black vinyl.

Models were introduced over the complete size range: the 320, 420, 520, 620, and 720 came in early to mid-1956, with the 820 following soon after. The 420s continued with the entire line of Model 40 tractors, including both a crawler and a Hi-Crop version. Although the tractors resembled the previous series from a distance, Deere's Sales Department had asked Henry Dreyfuss' designers for some new styling.

Dreyfuss knew of other ventures in the development and testing stages in Moline, Waterloo, and Dubuque. The scope of

these projects prohibited any large expenditures on current production, so Jim Connor, the Dreyfuss partner in charge of the John Deere account, recommended painting the engine cover's side panels in yellow, with contrasting dark green block letters for the John Deere name and lighter-weight script numbers for the model designation, which were to be placed on an angle down near the base of the radiator's side panel.

In 1958, this vertical side panel was trimmed back, the horizontal green bar eliminated, and the engine cover panel given a diagonal cut to further expose the engine. The tractor name remained in the same typeface, but the numbers, now identifying the 30 Series, were changed to shadow style and placed squarely onto the sheet metal near the top of the radiator. For the salespeople, that was change enough; it provided differences to point out to anyone who asked! If it were not for the paint, it would have been difficult otherwise to differentiate the 20 Series tractors from the new 330, 430, 530, 630, and 730 models.

Above: This 420 is used mostly for planting, harvesting, and hauling alfalfa.

Opposite page: Hi-Crops ran on 6x16 front tires and 12.4x38 rear tires. The 20 Series, such as this 620, came standard with Custom Powr-Trol and live PTO, each of which operated independently of the transmission clutch.

But Connor and his colleagues had been performing minor modifications to sheet metal and to instrument and control lever placement. And the 30 Series was yet a further visual tune-up for what was being developed behind the scenes.

If any tractors could be called pretty, they were the Models 530 and 630. With these machines, Dreyfuss' staff produced a truly stylish tractor. With their automobile-style dash panel behind a flipped-up cowl and with the steering wheel mounted flatter, more like an automobile's as well, the tractors reflected a functional

poise not seen before in industrial machine design. The flat, finely shaped rear fenders housed quad headlights, which were also the vogue among auto makers at that time. These fenders also incorporated a handgrip for ease in climbing onto or dismounting the tractors.

The seats benefited as well from still another stage of development. Dreyfuss had learned of the research done by Dr. Janet Travell at Harvard University Medical Center. Her work dealt with human engineering in a manner similar to Dreyfuss' own ideas. She had determined not only how to heal injuries to the lower back, but what caused them. And she had developed ideas about how to avoid them in the first place.

Travell had recently achieved some celebrity as a result of her orthopedic work on a young Massachusetts senator, John Kennedy. But her real work was much more than celebrity therapy. Her extensive research into back injuries and discomfort dovetailed with Dreyfuss' planned improvements to the tractor controls. Travell's studies led directly to the Float-Ride seat. This seat, introduced on the 20 Series, was given a shock absorber of its

(continued on page 169)

Above: This example is one of 17 produced that ran on all-fuel, using the 5.50x6.375-inch two-cylinder, which reached peak power at 1125 rpm.

Below: A Model 620 Orchard featuring streamlined protective bodywork.

Opposite page top: While the Model 40 tractors were succeeded by the 420s, this new series also provided about a 20 percent power increase as well as other features. But Sales and Marketing within Deere were aware of a market that still required the lesser power of the Model 40—in the 25 belt horsepower range—and they introduced the 320.

Opposite page bottom: Yellow vinyl seat covers made a big difference to the farmers who left their tractors in the sun to go home for midday dinner—the reflective color meant fewer burnt backsides. The 320 used the Model 40 four-speed transmission, with transport speed of 12 miles per hour and low gear, 1.5 miles per hour, capability of about 3,000 pounds from a 3,100-pound tractor.

Right: A 1957 Model Hi-Crop, number 6,215,383.

Opposite page: A 1958 Model 320 with asparagus box. The 320 was offered as Standard, Utility, Hi-Crop, and this V version, also known as the Southern Special, which fit midway between the Standard and Hi-Crop.

Above: Hydraulic controls were relocated to the side of the seat, available on either side if the farmer was left- or right-handed, and were placed to fit comfortably and naturally to the arm's motions. Dreyfuss' attention was to human factors, considerations that made the Deere tractors easier and safer to use.

Opposite page: The last two-cylinder John Deeres were introduced in 1959 with the 30 Series. These presented no engine or running gear changes but did introduce several styling and engineering ideas that Henry Dreyfuss Associates had developed at Deere's request to keep customer interest in advance of the New Generation. The 320s, in production from 1956–1958, were followed by the 330s, introduced in 1958 and carried on until 1960. Something like 1,090 were manufactured. This 1959 Standard, number 330,192, is owned by Bob Pollock of Denison, Iowa.

(continued on page 164)

own for the largest of the 30 Series tractors. Deere's operator comfort was unmatched by any other maker's.

In fact, the 30 Series tractors were as finely honed as any machines could be. When the 830 was introduced in mid-1959, the dealers, the branch agents, and the fortunate farmers invited to the premiere recognized that "this is just about as good as it gets." Deere & Company had advanced the art and science of hydraulic draft controls, engine breathing, operator comfort, and general ease of operation further than any other maker. Deere had introduced a weatherproof steel cab with good visibility and good ventilation. What's more, Deere had perfected the diesel engine to the highest art: At the end of 1959, a survey of the top five Nebraska Tractor Test performers—in terms of power and fuel economy—using any fuel, counted five Deere tractors. Sixth place, a Volvo, was 0.75 hp-hr/gal out of fifth. First place was Deere's 720 at 17.97 hp-hr/gal at 56.66 horsepower on belt.

By the middle of 1960, Deere & Company had built more than 1.45 million two-cylinder tractors. The tractor division had achieved breathtaking success. Tractors had gone from the single-most-dreaded topic of boardroom discussion to the corporate profit leader.

Loyal farmers, discontent only when crop prices fell or when machines failed to live up to expectations, had long since come to know and respect John Deere's tractors. With their power, their reliability, their ease of service, and their comfort, farmers had everything they wanted.

At that moment, so did Deere & Company. Because it had a secret, and it had a secret weapon. The secret was heading to Dallas, and the secret weapon was the man who had been present at the secret's birth, William Alexander Hewitt.

169

Above: The automobile-style sloping "dashboard" was a hint of things to come in 1960 but was offered to buyers in 1958 and 1959 on the 30 Series. The instrument cluster was completely redesigned by Henry Dreyfuss' designers for better visibility and easier reading.

Opposite page: Maurice Horn's 1959 Model 530 Standard, number 5,302,325, is part of his collection at Rochester, Indiana. Horn's fully optioned and beautifully restored 530 shows off the best of Dreyfuss and Deere's efforts at hinting to the farmer the future appearance and features to be offered on the John Deere agricultural tractors.

Above: Engine and running gear for the Model 530 were those of the 520, which had been tested at the University of Nebraska in late 1956. The engine was Deere's 4.69x5.50-inch horizontal two-cylinder. Drawbar horsepower was rated at 26.1 while 36.1 horsepower were produced on the belt pulley at 1325 rpm. The Model 530 weighed 4,960 shipped from Waterloo.

Left: The adjustable seat had its own shock absorber to smooth the ride. Hydraulic adjustments literally fell to hand as Dreyfuss' Human Factors engineering placed all the operational controls within easy reach. The platform—the floor—was cleaned up for comfort while sitting or standing.

Opposite page: The last Dreyfuss clean-up on two-cylinder Deere tractors was really the trial run for the back-end design of the New Generation tractors. Dual rear hydraulic systems, which allowed the farmer great flexibility, were located by Dreyfuss so as to appear logical and obvious as to their purpose and operation

The New Generation of Power was introduced in Dallas on August 30, 1960, to nearly 6,000 John Deere dealers, distributors, and friends. After a seven-year gestation, the secret was out. After 40 years of repudiating four- and six-cylinder engines, John Deere's surprise was total! When the crowd left Dallas, most were already sold on the new machines.

CHAPTER 18

A New Generation of Power
Deere's Surprise

"Every farmer is a born mechanic," Bill Hewitt observed. There was no judgment in this; his tone of voice did not poke fun. Far from it. He spoke as though he was pointing out an important perspective from which to view Deere's history.

He was. It is.

"And the two-cylinder tractor was the essence of simplicity," he continued. "The good farmer could do a lot of the repairs on it.

"If he needed to have the valves ground or the cylinders bored, all he had to do was remove the engine block and take it in to the dealer. And the dealer would send it to the company branch house. There were already other people's cylinder blocks which had been ground. These were waiting for immediate transfer.

"You didn't have to send your block in and wait to have it ground. You sent it in and immediately got an exchanged one for it.

"Those were the kinds of things," he explained, "that kept tractors running, because the two-cylinder model was so easy for a normally talented farmer-mechanic to keep running. He could put in the gaskets and do everything that was needed for repair. Even the absence of a self-starter made it easier!"

As Deere & Company approached its 100th anniversary in 1937, Hewitt was approaching graduation from the University of California at Berkeley. He had majored in economics. The native San Franciscan had given little thought to agricultural implements. He had grown up in a cosmopolitan city, and he was regularly exposed to its cultural opportunities.

While Hewitt studied supply and demand, farmers' demand of tractor power was met with an industry average of around 35 horsepower. Rubber tires, introduced to the farm in Hewitt's last year of high school, had a real effect on the microeconomy of the farm by 1937. But it was not much longer before the macroeconomic lessons of World War II returned tractors to steel. The War Production Board practiced a supply-and-demand economics of its own.

Hewitt graduated from Berkeley in 1937 and went east to Harvard Business School. A year later, as Deere & Company turned 101, Hewitt returned to California, his own economy coming up short of funds to continue his postgraduate study. After some time as an accountant for Standard Oil of California and more time as an advertising writer for a men's clothing maker, the Second World War sent him to sea. Soon after Pearl Harbor's invasion, Hewitt boarded a battleship called USS *California*. When the war ended four years later, Lieutenant Commander Hewitt returned to California and then entered the farm machinery business, working as a territory manager for a Ford tractor distributorship.

In 1948, he married, and a few months later, his father-in-law offered him a job. Hewitt, a talented manager for Ford, was a hot prospect for the Deere & Company family. He was someone many people saw as having a bright future. And he was by then already a part of the Deere's family: he had married Patricia Wiman, daughter of Colonel Charles Deere Wiman.

Hewitt exceeded expectations, and, as he learned rapidly, he rose through the company. Joining Deere as territory manager for the San Francisco branch office, he was promoted first to assistant branch manager and then to manager, all the while learning from Ben

"Engineers are machine oriented; the goodness of Dreyfuss' work is how the human interfaces with the machine. For Dreyfuss, this meant safer, more comfortable, more efficient, more convenient."

—Jim Connor

Above: Introduced during "Flight 63," the new 20 Series tractors boasted many new features. Synchro Range and Power Shift transmissions were offered. The instrument pod nestled beneath a cowl inspired by the automobile and strongly influenced by Dreyfuss' Human Factors. The seat slid out of the way for better access when standing at the wheel.

Opposite page: From nose to tail, features and details for the Grove and Orchard tractors came from the minds of Deere engineering in Waterloo and Moline and from Henry Dreyfuss' designers, at that time working in Pasadena, California. Larger engines required more cooling capability, but so many other features had to be contained within the tractor that the challenges were endless.

Keator, a man of proven perception. It was Keator, along with Pat Murphy, who had led Lindeman into the Deere family as well.

Wiman watched his son-in-law but did not pave Hewitt's way. Hewitt earned his own stripes, gaining a reputation for sensitivity, grace, even-handedness, intelligence, and fairness. In a company such as Deere, these virtues were also part of the firm's legacy.

In 1954, when Colonel Wiman was diagnosed as terminally ill with only a short time remaining, he left it for others to nominate his son-in-law to be his successor. And Keator did just that.

In a letter to Wiman, quoted by Wayne Broehl in *John Deere's Company*, Keator's endorsement fairly glowed: "We should have a young man—this is most important—who is a leader, who knows the business and has a vision for the future of our line, who is cognizant of the problems to be met and how to handle them. . . .

"He has youth," Keator continued, warming to the task of supporting his first protégé, "he is smart, catches on to things quick, and has vision, enthusiasm, and courage to get things done. . . . He has had a broad field to operate in and had the authority to act. This is important if he is to be able to face up to the task. . . .

"Bill," Keator summed up, "is a very dignified and personable man and you would go a long way before you would find his equal for that job."

Wiman's health continued to deteriorate. On June 22, 1954, setting up the succession, he created a new position, executive vice president, and he nominated Hewitt to fill it. The board vote was unanimous. Not quite 11 months later, on May 12, 1955, Wiman died, and on May 24, Hewitt, not quite 41 years of age, was elected Deere & Company's sixth president.

"At that time," Hewitt recalled 38 years later, "my predecessor had already started the design work for the New Generation of Power four- and six-cylinder tractors. When Deere & Company celebrated its 100th birthday, the industry nationwide was producing tractors with, on average, 35 horsepower. Remember, after World War II, with the advent of hydraulic systems [came] the three-point hitch, which Harry Ferguson developed. . . . Tractors had additional hydraulic systems to attach to plows and disk harrows to raise them and lower them. It got to the point where it took 35 horsepower just to run the hydraulic systems!

"That was a momentous change, this New Generation of Power. Because the way they [Deere's engineers] described it was, they started with clean sheets of paper on a drawing board.

"Up until then, most of the 'improvements' were improvements which modified the previous design. And the 'improved' design came out, and later it was 'improved.' But each time, it was modifications."

Those who had done the modifications, as Bill Hewitt knew well, were his engineers at Deere & Company and Deere's designers at Henry Dreyfuss Associates. For those engineers and designers, however, the clean sheets of paper represented a starting point from which many things were possible.

"The Waterloo people," Jim Connor began, "had already come up with a design and a kind of mockup tractor when we got into this New Generation of Power project." Connor, a design partner with Dreyfuss, had joined Henry Dreyfuss Associates in 1952. He was the man in charge of design from the firm's office for the New Generation tractors.

"Wisely, at Waterloo," Connor continued, "they had taken a task force out of the group concerned with day-to-day engineering, and removed them to a separate place to work on the new tractors. The Falls Avenue Annex, at Falls and Knoll Avenue, was an abandoned grocery store, which the company rented. This prototype mockup was of interest to us as a kind of starting point, but we quickly discarded it.

"It had a narrow-angle V-6 engine in it. I don't know if they ever built running engines. It was pretty slim, but still, the valve covers protruded some into the line of sight. There were no doubt other considerations too, because the V-6 engine went away rather soon. We also had some concerns."

Henry Dreyfuss Associates' concerns were the same ones it had held for years—the "human factors": how to make any project with which it was involved more operator friendly. As Connor explained it,

(continued on page 181)

Above: This 1965 Diesel Model 3020 Grove and Orchard, number 81,139, has a four-cylinder engine, with 4.25x4.75-inch bore and stroke, produced 57.1 horsepower on the drawbar and 65.3 horsepower on the PTO at 2500 rpm in Nebraska Tests. Standard Model 3020s weighed 9,585 pounds for tests, without additional Orchard bodywork.

Left: A 1966 4020 with Roll-Gard at work in the field.

"The curved hood started with the New Generation tractors. Henry proposed—and stuck to—the idea of making the tractor hood one piece. 'They do it for automobiles,' he said. 'They stamp the entire roof of a car! So let's do this as a one-piece hood."

Above: Dr. Janet Travell's improved seat was one development farmers appreciated first. It featured back lumbar area support as well as armrests and middle-back support. The instrument panel boasted simplified instrumentation, clearly readable whether seated or standing. All gear and throttle indications were cleaned up.

Left: This workhorse 1965 Model 4020, number 94,255, sits in as field fitted with Deere's chisel plow to break up some soil. Built in Waterloo, the 4020 and 3020 became mainstays of Deere's tractor lineup from 1965 until the introduction of the Generation II tractors in 1972.

(continued from page 177)

"Engineers are machine oriented; the goodness of Dreyfuss' work is how the human interfaces with the machine." For Dreyfuss, this meant safer, more comfortable, more efficient, more convenient. These were improvements his designers had consistently sought to achieve from previous designs for production tractors.

"Our approach was not streamlining," Connor explained. "It was to make a nice-looking tractor where everything had its reason for being.

"The curved hood started with the New Generation tractors. Henry proposed—and stuck to—the idea of making the tractor hood one piece. Instead of it being a lot of little pieces welded together, he wanted it made as one piece. 'They do it for automobiles,' he said. 'They stamp the entire roof of a car! So let's do this as a one-piece hood.'

"He had a reason. There were a lot of tire and wheel options on these tractors. And sometimes, you had bigger wheels in the front so the tractor would be pointed uphill. Sometimes, it would be the other way, pointed downhill. We never could tell what the buyer would want for his particular operation.

"By having a curved line on top," Connor went on, "you couldn't so easily tell that the tractor was leaning one way or another. And later, with the Sound-Gard cabs, we tapered with cab windows. So there was no longer any vertical or horizontal reference line in the side profile. It didn't look funny—or like it was broken—when it was tilted down or up in the field!"

Such detail seems inconsequential until Deere is compared with the competition. Dreyfuss' organization was very aware that most tractor purchases involved the whole family. If Deere & Company tractors were the mechanical equal to International Harvester's or Ford's, and if Deere's looked better—less "funny"—pulling plows in the field or running home down the road for dinner, then that might cinch a sale.

The tilt of the tractor had another effect. It called to Dreyfuss' attention the question of farmers' comfort and ease of operating the controls.

Dreyfuss had opened an office in Pasadena, California, in 1945, and by 1953, when Deere approached his firm about the New Generation tractors, all the Deere work was being done in California. The former Killefer Manufacturing Corporation works were still Deere & Company facilities in Los Angeles. Killefer,

The new Model 4020 used Deere's six-cylinder 4.252x4.75-inch engine. At the University of Nebraska, the tractor rated 78.0 drawbar and 91.2 PTO horsepower at 2200 rpm. In test trim, it tipped the scales at 13,055 pounds and towed 10,184 pounds. It was one of the first Deere tractors to exceed a $10,000 list price: its suggested retail was $10,345.

acquired by Deere in 1937, produced heavy-duty tillage equipment, and always had new tractors on hand for testing implements. So Connor and Dreyfuss' senior partner Bill Purcell made the short trip from the Pasadena office to Los Angeles to study one of the current production tractors.

"We made a whole bunch of photographs of Bill working the controls," Connor explained. "A lot was still unchanged from the old Model B. We had Bill going through all the motions. Depicting all the things that were wrong with the tractor, that made it difficult to operate in terms of human factors. From those photos, we began to figure out from our knowledge of ergonomics all the things we needed to change.

"One was the angle of the steering wheel, to make it less vertical. Location of the pedals. Location of the levers. This was all aimed toward the New Generation of Power. But we developed a lot of this stuff quickly, and Deere knew that the new tractor was due to be introduced in 1960—and here we were in 1956. They wanted to upgrade their current tractors between then and the introduction. They wanted to keep the existing tractors alive and selling.

"We cleaned up the operator's platform, we relocated controls and instruments, narrowed the cowl at the back even more—with the cast-iron cowl and instrument pod—for greater visibility while the farmer was cultivating. We introduced flat fenders with handgrips and headlights.

"One thing we introduced on the New Generation was the Human Factor seat. One of my first assignments when I started with Dreyfuss was to work on the Lockheed Electra in 1953 and 1954. We worked very closely with Dr. Janet Travell on the airplane seats. When Henry got Travell in to do a study of tractor seats and to work with us, she went out to Waterloo to drive tractors.

"And she turned up," Connor began to laugh, "in the field, on the morning we were going to do this, wearing green slacks and a yellow top. I think the engineers were intrigued, because of the fact that Henry brought her in with Bill Hewitt's blessing. We developed a seat based on her study.

"It had an interesting innovation. Dr. Travell knew that as your stature increases, your legs get longer and you want to be further away and your arms are longer. She figured out an angle—about 27 degrees—so that the seat went up and down on an inclined track. And we developed a suspension with springs and dampers—shock absorbers—that could be adjusted for the weight of the operator. And, it had a memory." Connor laughed out loud, amused even now by the technological marvels that appeared on Deere's tractors but that automakers would not adopt for another two decades.

"She [Dr. Travell] was quite taken with the fact that tractors run over rough ground. She figured you didn't want too much pressure on the front of the seat, that you wanted to brace with your feet. So the front seat was tipped downward slightly. The idea was you braced yourself in the seat and you actually helped hold yourself in! The seat had a back where the arms and back curved around. The back was designed to include lumbar support. There was an upper back support above that on a spring."

Connor, who retired in 1987 after 35 years with Dreyfuss, still marveled over the seat he and Travell had developed. He had taken her findings and ideas and made them work. The seat's success still

pleased him. His work had advanced tractor comfort by years, and it took the competition years to catch up. Connor and Dreyfuss' relationship with Deere & Company was part of the reason such advances were possible.

"We never took the design problem," he explained "and ran home with it and did it all up and brought it back and said, 'This is it! This is the way it's going to be.'

"Everything we did was on a cooperative and mutual basis. Our whole philosophy from Henry right through the organization, was to have everybody involved so that it's approved in little pieces all the way along until the whole thing comes out.

"The interesting thing about Bill Hewitt was that he took a personal interest in all the products. He would be there. If we were showing a new prototype, he would come. He would look at it. He would check it out pretty thoroughly. If he had comments, he would walk up to Henry or Bill or me. He would always compliment us first. And then he might mention a question or a concern about some detail or some element. More often than not, what he had to say was really well worth listening to, and not just because he was the president of the company. He had a good aesthetic sense, and his impressions were quite valid. Really right there."

This made for the other element of Dreyfuss' success with Deere & Company. Keeping everyone—engineering, manufacturing, sales, and marketing—in the flow of information and allowing them equal access at every stage eliminated any possibility of problems on the eve of production. "We can't do that" or "We don't have tools that can stretch this metal or bend that piece" was never heard at the last minute. Hewitt's own close interest and involvement meant that approval came from the top down. All the steps necessary from the prototype show through product manufacture to introduction and service in the marketplace represented no surprises to—or from—anyone involved.

Until D-day, August 29, 1960.

That Monday, more than 100 airplanes from 75 cities delivered nearly 6,000 John Deere dealers and spouses to Dallas. The next day, when Hewitt opened the back door of the convention center and all the faithful filed out, they saw $2 million worth of New Generation of Power, 136 tractors and 324 supplementary machines spread across a 15-acre parking lot next to the Cotton Bowl Stadium.

Having not known what to expect—but, after years of company denials, certainly not anticipating four- and six-cylinder engines—the dealers were astounded.

D-day, August 29, 1960: More than 100 airplanes from 75 cities delivered nearly 6,000 John Deere dealers and spouses to Dallas. The next day, when Hewitt opened the back door of the convention center and all the faithful filed out, they saw $2 million worth of New Generation of Power, 136 tractors and 324 supplementary machines spread across a 15-acre parking lot next to the Cotton Bowl Stadium. The dealers were astounded.

This 1989 Model 8760 chops a 31-foot swath with a Model 635 disk harrow across corn stubble.

CHAPTER 19

Generation II Tractors
The Search for More Power, the Quest for More Features

The New Generation of Power in 1960 introduced multicylinder tractors ranging from the 80-horsepower six-cylinder diesel 4010 down to the 35-horsepower four-cylinder gas or diesel 1010. By 1962, the line had been supplemented with the 5010, a 100-horsepower, seven-bottom-plow-rated, six-cylinder two-wheel-drive tractor. In addition, an orchard-and-grove version of the small 1010 and of the 55-horsepower four-cylinder 3010 were available. But neither Deere nor Dreyfuss was resting on their newly earned laurels.

Three years after D-day in Dallas, Deere & Company organized Flight 63, to bring the same dealers to Waterloo. Sales had settled slightly, and company management had two goals for this visit: First, showing distributors the factory and the tractors on the production line might spark dealer incentive. Second, if that didn't do it, the introduction of two new models might. The 3020 increased power from 59 horsepower to 65 horsepower out of the four-cylinder engine, and the 4020 raised the already respectable output of the six from 84 horsepower to 91 horsepower. To get the power to the ground, the company offered an optional Power Differential Lock.

In 1965, the 5010 was upgraded to 5020 nomenclature, its power increased from 121 horsepower to 133 horsepower. In 1969, its output was increased again, to 141 horsepower. Still, the competition for power continued. The 4020 and the 3020 were offered with optional hydraulic-powered front-wheel-drive, which was not yet a four-wheel-drive, but provided a marked increase in traction. And, with modifications inside the engine, power increased again, to 96 horsepower for the 4020 and 71 horsepower for the four-cylinder 3020. Another generation of

"Always, though, we preserved the principles. They don't change. Integrity doesn't change. Certain methods change, to adapt to changing forces that surface themselves in the passage of time."

—Bill Hewitt

power was reached with the introduction of turbochargers on the diesel 4020 model, renumbered the 4520 in 1968, with 122 horsepower; the 4320 arrived in 1971 with 115 horsepower, and the 4620 superseded the 4520 with 135 horsepower. These looked virtually identical to the first New Generation tractors, except that their front tires were smaller, chevron-patterned versions of the rears and the front axles boasted substantial reinforcement in front of and around the differential housing.

In 1968, the four-wheel-drive replacement for the 8010 and 8020 was introduced, as the 7020, with 145 horsepower. Three years later, the 7520 arrived with 175 horsepower. With power still in demand, another new generation was imminent.

But six years into the life of the New Generation, at approximately its halfway point, Henry Dreyfuss Associates' efforts with human factors produced a very unpopular option. Getting the farmer to accept it was Deere's most difficult marketing chore. It took gift offerings at trade shows, and then a major corporate giveaway.

Farmers understood the logic behind rollover protection. They just believed that the need for it would never be theirs. Deere's Roll-Gard structure was offered for sale in 1966, and even enhanced with a roof, it met few takers.

Bill Hewitt recalled the resistance and the steps the company took to make the safety device more appealing to the invincible farmers. "We made a significant contribution to operator safety and comfort," he began. "The most tractor operator fatalities occur when the tractor rolls over. But in designing a roll bar, it's not just something where you put a bar over the top. You have to test it and engineer it."

"To install a proper roll bar would add $500 or $800 to the cost of the tractor. But instead of paying $800 more for a Deere tractor, they would buy another tractor over there. Because farmers—being human—knew that they didn't need a roll bar.

"So," Hewitt said with a rueful smile, "we solved the problem this way: We decided to give all of our engineering specs to each of our competitors. They wouldn't have to go through the process of testing and developing. . . . on the agreement that they would make roll bars standard equipment and we would make them standard equipment.

"Because we couldn't sell the things in any quantity to justify our investment in them, we gave away our engineering." Hewitt paused to let the significance sink in.

By 1966, Deere & Company was no longer content to be runner-up. In fact, it was no longer runner-up. In a gesture that attended to the "human factors" in a way rarely duplicated in American business history, Hewitt gave away to his runners-up the millions of dollars and nearly six years worth of research Deere & Company had prepared in the interest of operator safety.

"Everybody then adopted roll bars," he laughed. "Then, the cabs came in with glass and air conditioning, and the roll bar was incorporated, and we couldn't make them fast enough."

"The Roll-Gard came first," Jim Connor picked up the story from the Henry Dreyfuss Associates perspective. "That was roll structure. They [Deere & Company] couldn't give it away. They wanted to make their tractors safer, being tuned into 'human factors'—somewhat due to Henry Dreyfuss, but certainly due to their own concern.

"The farmer wouldn't buy them. They took them to farm shows, trade fairs, tractor expos, and the wives began to see them.

They became the deciding factor. The wives didn't want their husbands killed in tractor accidents.

"Deere gave them away as raffle prizes, door prizes. Gave them away!

"When we started on the Generation II tractors, the brief we worked out together was to make the Roll-Gard and the cab integrated. So that the structure of the cab was strong enough to take a roll over. That was the beginning of the Sound-Gard cab."

Connor smiled proudly. The Sound-Gard had been his project, his baby. Its appearance, its testing, its development, its first introduction to Deere's engineers were all at his direction.

"It was decided that we were going to do the best cab possible, that it was going to have all the safety features, all the human factors features that a cab could have: rollover protection; sound insulation; heat insulation; operator insulation from vibration and dust; air conditioning; pressurization so the air goes out, does not get sucked in; improved vision; easy entry and exit; flat platform;

the second generation of the Travell-designed seat. That cab on the Generation II tractors just blew everybody away."

Including, especially, two Deere & Company engineers and several of Connor's colleagues.

"We built the mockup out of plywood and two-by-fours. Engineering had told us where the posts had to be and how big. We figured out where the door would open on the front, and we had a big windshield, made out of a couple pieces of plexiglass, with a roof mockup." Connor smiled as he continued his story. He had prefaced it by explaining that it concerned the day he almost got fired by Dreyfuss.

"We had this mounted on a tractor, were ready to show it to the two engineers this one particular morning. One was the head of the project, the other his assistant. The night before, I had an inspiration.

"'Why don't we make this a little more dramatic,' I said to Henry. Henry loved the dramatic. His house in Pasadena was up on a knoll, [and] the 'barn' (actually, it was a large carriage house where we worked) was down a long, curved driveway below the house—and hidden from it.

"'Let's have the tractor up at the house, and we'll drive it down the driveway so they can see it from a distance, see it coming, build up some drama.'

"Henry was a little reluctant but finally agreed. The person working on the cab with me was Chuck Pelle, so Chuck was going to drive the tractor down the hill."

Connor smiled again.

"But Chuck was not a tractor driver. We got the two engineers down to the barn. I'm there, Bill Purcell is there, Henry is there, so I ran back up the drive and waved to Chuck, then ran back down and heard the diesel start up.

"And I thought he sounded like he was coming pretty fast. And he was. He was in transport gear. And he was going downhill. . . .

"Well, he came around the curve, into sight, and then we all suddenly realized that there was a Volkswagen parked inside the curve, against the embankment, heading up the hill, just out of Chuck's line of sight."

Connor started to chuckle now, more than 20 years after the fact.

"Chuck came down the hill, came tearing down the hill. At the last minute, he saw the Volkswagen, tried to avoid it. Didn't. His left rear wheel rode up over the fender of the Volkswagen. The tractor, which was a tricycle, tilted way over. And then it slammed down. Thank God, it didn't tip over.

"But it slammed down. This mockup cab pitched hard. The plexiglass windshield flew out and shattered. The battery for the tractor—which we had undone and just left sitting on the step, fell off and was dragged along the ground.

"Chuck managed to get the thing stopped about 10 feet from the barn. He was as white as a sheet. For good reason. He got out and just kept looking from the cab to us, to the cab, to us."

Connor now started to laugh.

"Henry calmly walked over to the tractor. He didn't say anything to Chuck—not, 'My God! Chuck! You nearly got killed!'

"No, Mr. Cool just walked over and started doing the presentation like this was the plan. Those two engineers, who knew this was right on the brink of disaster, stood there wide-eyed, their mouths open. Henry just stood there, so cool as if nothing unusual had happened, and went right on with the presentation. So these two guys looked at each other and then they kind of got into it."

Connor was now laughing hugely.

"Afterwards, Henry took me aside and said to me, 'There will be no more tractor driving by any of our people any more.' It was one of the highlights of my career!" Connor said, still enjoying his history.

The Sound-Gard, having survived its engineering introduction, received the engineers' blessing and once in production, was offered on all four of the Generation II tractors introduced on August 19, 1972, in New Orleans. The appearance of the tractors changed with the hood adopted by Henry Dreyfuss Associates' next-generation ideas.

"The down-sloping hood," Connor explained, "which came out on the 1972 tractors, from a design standpoint had a couple things going for it.

"One, to let it slope downward gave you better visibility over the nose. Two, it gave you more space under the back of the hood to get 'stuff' in—where you always have more trouble and need more space, because there is more 'stuff' that needs to be in there. So we brought the back up, front down, and curved the top. Now, there was no

longer a 'horizontal' horizon line to look at, to sight along. It picked up what we started with the tractors in 1960."

Nomenclature picked up what had been started with the New Generation as well. The new 4030 offered 80 horsepower, the 4230 offered 100 horsepower, the 4430 produced 125 horsepower, and the 4630 rated 150 horsepower at the PTO. Synchro-Range transmissions were standard, connected by the Perma-Clutch, a hydraulic wet-plate clutch. For the farmer needing even more power, the articulated four-wheel drives boasted 175 horsepower from the 8430 and 225 horsepower from the 8630.

With the Generation II tractors, Deere's tractor engineering and Dreyfuss' human engineering put power at the finger tips of the farmer in unprecedented amounts and with unmatched sophistication. It also put the competition a generation behind.

At the same time, Bill Hewitt led Deere & Company out of the United States and into the world to find new customers and new markets, and to create new products for them. He gave Deere's domestic tractor customers what his predecessors had promised would never come: four- and six-cylinder engines. Almost immediately after introduction of these larger engines, the customers

Above: A 1989 8760 with a 635 disk. The 8760 produced 240.2 drawbar and 256.9 PTO horsepower at 2100 rpm out of its turbocharged and intercooled six-cylinder 5.12x5.00-inch diesel. At 2100 rpm—5.4 miles per hour—a quarter section was disked in less than eight hours.

Opposite page: A 1984 2750. Deere introduced its 50 series two years earlier.

flocked to the New Generation with a devotion and enthusiasm unexpected—and unparalleled in the history of American industry.

"Always, though, we preserved the principles," Hewitt explained. "They don't change. Integrity doesn't change. Certain methods change, to adapt to changing forces that surface themselves in the passage of time."

For Deere & Company, one force was a phone call from Hewitt's father-in-law, Charles Deere Wiman, to offer Hewitt the chance of his life. For Hewitt and Deere & Company, the force was a sheet of paper. At the bottom of the page was a line that can now be highlighted in green:

"Not content to be runner-up."

Index